Excellent Oral and Written Communication Skills Required

A Guidebook for Career Advancement

Tom Stapleton

Stapleton Communications
1018 Marengo Drive
Glendale, CA 91206
(626) 792-2058
StapComm@aol.com

© 1994, 1996, 1999, 2002 Tom Stapleton

First printing, October 1994
Second printing, November 1996
Third printing, March 1999
Fourth printing, August 2002

ISBN 0-9643217-4-2

This book is fondly dedicated to my wife, Jean, without whose help I never would have been able to figure out how to use WordPerfect in preparing the text. She also graciously assisted with proofreading.

I am deeply grateful to Gerry Holst for his technical assistance in text formatting and layout.

Any errors or omissions in the text are fully my responsibility, as much as I would prefer to lay blame on someone else.

Printing and binding by Pace Lithographers, Inc., City of Industry, CA

Cover artwork by Crystal Stephens

Table of Contents

Table of Contents

Excellent Oral and Written
Communication Skills Required

October 1987 was a significant month for America. Not only did the stock market crash then, but results of a most important survey were published, results charting a course for your career advancement through the 1990's . . . and well beyond.

That month's edition of <u>Business Forum</u> magazine, published by California State University–Los Angeles, included the results of a survey conducted by the University of North Carolina. Two hundred American CEO's were asked which abilities promotable employees must demonstrate to ensure successful career pathing. The chart below presents the answers:

SURVEY OF CHIEF EXECUTIVES	
<u>Key Learning Area</u>	Rank
Oral & Written Communication Skills	1
Interpersonal Skills	2
Financial Managerial Account Skills	3
The Ability to Think, be Analytical, and Make Decisions	4
Strategic Planning & Goal Setting	5
Motivation & Commitment	6
Understanding of Economics	7
MIS & Computer Applications	8
Knowledge of Business, Culture and Overall Environment	9
Marketing Concept	10
Integrity	11
Setting Short & Long Term Career Objectives	12
Leadership Skills	13
Understanding Business Functions	14
Time Management	15

Are you surprised that Oral and Written Communication Skills rank highest? You shouldn't be. Just check the help–wanted ads for supervisory or managerial positions in the Business or Classified sections of any metropolitan newspaper, and you'll see the same phrase time and again: "Excellent oral and written communication skills required." Especially in today's service economy, employability is judged — and advancement based — largely on how well thoughts are articulated. That's true whether you're writing a report, updating a résumé, or conducting a management briefing.

Yet, as a communications consultant, the question I hear over and over again is, "How come they don't teach us this in school?" Invariably, the query is posed by otherwise well-educated corporate or public-sector achievers, men and women designated by their Human Resources department as candidates for my workshop because they've never quite learned how to communicate clear, forceful messages that get results.

And all the while, more ill-prepared graduates pour into the workplace where their written documents, awash in gobbledygook, fall flat. Their proposals go unresponded to, failing to sell. Their presentations fizzle, unable to stimulate or problem solve. Think what flawed impressions these ineffective messages convey.

Okay, then . . . how come they don't teach us this in school? The answer is fairly simple, yet startling. Schools, beyond the elementary grades, aren't in the business of teaching skills. They teach subjects. And it's not so much learning which occurs as conditioning. Employers rightfully expect that new hires be solidly grounded in the requisite subject matter, but all too quickly the boss finds communication aptitude woefully lacking. The upshot: non-productive messages going from sender to receiver without passing through the mind of either, in constipated communication styles devoid of "audience-friendly" qualities.

Then the calls go out to training consultants, people otherwise typically joked about as "someone from out of town with slides," or "someone who knows 50 ways of making love but can't get any dates." Skill development is left until late in the game — left to adult education specialists who face the daunting task of trying to undo the damage. It's like trying to unring a bell.

The solution seems simple, right? Expand the schools' curricula to teach skills as well as subjects. Well, it's already being done, and it's a laudable development. Many public education systems are working on restoring the three R's through back-to-basic movements, teacher upgrading, and other amelioration tactics.

Still, part of the answer to "how come?" lies in the reality that skills simply don't enjoy the same status as subjects. An invidious culprit lurks behind this wrongheaded skill bashing, namely, the type of mentality which holds that education in communications proficiency is somehow a second-rate offering on the traditional syllabus.

This attitude is particularly troubling when it finds a voice in, for example, a recent national newsmagazine article on education. There the author sniped that English courses have deemphasized the teaching of literature, stressing "language arts" — or communication skills — instead, and bemoaned the fact that students can get credit for a business communications course.

What's more, George F. Will, a usually erudite social critic of considerable national standing, not long ago belittled in print what he termed the "thin gruel of language arts" which stress communications now being taught in schools.

How come there's something declassé about learning to communicate? Must we somehow merchandise the ability before it catches on, commercialize it as a must item of acquisition, like trendy cars, designer clothing, or fiber-rich diets? God knows, there is a market for the skill (or consultants like me wouldn't be in business). But certain influential segments of society just haven't been sold yet on the need to make an attitude adjustment.

What's needed is more understanding like that displayed by the respondents to the University of North Carolina survey. (Incidentally, subsequent surveys of senior executives, published in US News & World Report in June 1990, and in Working in October 1993, also rank communication skills at or near the top.)

All of us, and not just CEO's or senior executives, have a responsibility to promote such an attitude adjustment, continually making sure — in fact, *demanding* — that meat and not merely gristle is being sold in our schools. For instance, I spend inordinate amounts of workshop time trying to get participants to dispose of much excess baggage they unwittingly lug into adulthood. Like,

"Never begin a sentence with a conjunction such as 'because' or 'like.'" Or, "Never end a sentence with a preposition." (Which reminds me of the apocryphal response of the Irish writer Bernard Shaw when English Prime Minister Winston Churchill reputedly criticized him for ending a sentence with a preposition in a telegram. Shaw cabled back: "Your arrant attitude is one up with which I will not put.")

We learned these arbitrary rules at impressionable ages, and the lessons often stuck. Others, deemed important at the time, didn't take. Consider that the typical American gradeschooler learns four types of sentences in English: simple, compound, complex, and compound-complex. (Your brain is probably shifting into park at this point. Well, how do you suppose the gradeschooler feels?)

In nearly eighteen years of conducting my seminars I've met only the rare adult who can define — or even cares — what a compound-complex sentence is. Yet, the "basics" (English, math, history, science, et. al.) are overloaded with such arcane convolutions. With gristle. What's more helpful to know about sentences in the political world of work is how to find or phrase the main idea and what its implications are.

So why do they bother teaching us stuff that we really don't need to know? I've got a theory. Studying things like subordinate clauses and correlative conjunctions is boring, exasperating, often pointless. Just like much of adult life. So it's good future training!

Most of us who make our way through the educational system are confused, especially employees and employers. On the one hand, we're trying to reverse the disheartening trend of a nation educationally and culturally at risk by reinforcing a policy of teaching core subjects. But the hard evidence, once we begin drawing a paycheck, is that it's all not enough. Only then do we learn perhaps the most important lesson of all: performance and promotion are critical functions of an ability to communicate efficiently — a highly sought-after skill. Management consultants across the land are telling us that there is no such thing as job security anymore. In an era of increased downsizing (or "rightsizing" as it's also commonly referred to), the only lasting security lies in developing skills employers want.

This is a book about skills. It's also about style. I believe strongly that, while skills may be difficult to teach, they can be learned. And the way to stimulate that learning is to make it enjoyable, challenging, and rewarding. Understanding the way skills are applied means taking into account the role of style: what it is and how it distinguishes — in every sense of the word — your communications.

I'm not going to try to talk you into liking having to write a report or get up in front of people and speak. Only how to make the processes as straight ahead and painless as possible. I'll lace my message with sprinklings of Business English, human psychology, maybe even a little Zen — all in an attempt to demystify the language and make proficiency in using it more accessible to *you*, the leaders of the 21st Century.

If you've never done well in English courses, take heart. This book is for you. If you've managed to earn a degree without once having to satisfy the public speaking requirement — and now wish you had — take heart. If facing the task of having to compose even a routine memo or speak to a small group of co-workers strikes fear and loathing into the core of your being, take heart. Even if you're a classic "message procrastinator" who puts off (or completely avoids) any engagement of interpersonal communication, there is help. That's what this book is all about.

In the best sense, it's a self-help book. You'll find workable procedures in these pages for getting your thoughts across. To help you make the most of the information contained within, each chapter is simply organized to present an overview of the subject matter, then necessary details, and finally summary information on the significant ideas presented. You'll find material cross-referenced where appropriate to amplify discussion and assist your understanding of the subject matter. And I've included checklists to provide at-a-glance comprehension.

No matter how much you may have already read on the topic of improving business or personal communications, no matter how experienced a writer or speaker you may have already become, you'll find this book a wealth of new information, presented in a readily absorbed and easily practiced manner. It's true that there's always room for improvement regardless of the level of proficiency you now enjoy (or seek to rise to).

This book is designed to help you enhance or develop skills necessary for continued success in the workplace and in personal dealings. It represents eighteen years of effort on my part in digging out, sorting out, and trying out which methods really get the message-sending job done. And that translates into *results* if you'll try putting the information to work.

Keep in mind that effective communications are those the reader or listener understands and responds to. Your messages will achieve those ends only as a direct function of your willingness and ability to think them through, refining your efforts as you proceed, and then measuring your effectiveness. There is no magic wand that I (or anyone else) can wave to make an achiever out of you. To change behavior for the better requires:

1) Wanting very strongly to improve

and

2) Working very hard at improving

These are steps that will work whether you're trying to quit smoking, lose weight, get that promotion — or become more proficient at oral and written communication skills.

Think about what your expectations are as you begin reading this book, what goals you hope to attain by the time you've finished. You can best achieve only when you have a clear purpose in mind.

So that's your first step: to know why you think reading this book, and practicing its precepts, will be of benefit. Then, be willing to enter into a partnership with me. I'll lead you through all the book's performance standards, guiding and explaining as you proceed, so that you can work at your own pace in learning how to diagnose and remedy communication deficiencies — how to, in effect, become your own toughest critic and satisfactorily choose a specific manner by which you'll improve your oral and written communication skills.

It's been said that life is like a tuba: you get out of it what you put into it. The same is true of any learning experience. Be willing to invest time and effort — to invest of yourself and *concentrate* on the task at hand — and you'll reap dividends.

You may be wondering, since I mentioned schools and the educational system earlier, whether this book will be merely another academic experience for you, like an assigned "text" you must complete for a teacher's approval. No, I won't be taking you down any classroom memory lanes, though you will get exposure to refresher information. I assure you, I'm not an academic, and this book won't read like one of those dry, dull grammar handbooks you found so distasteful early on in life. I'm convinced that one of the reasons English courses, in fact the entire subject matter of oral and written communications, is such a turn-off for so many adults is that they remember dry, dull, underwhelming teachers using dry, dull, underwhelming textbooks.

You can probably easily recall those *dear old golden rule days* now, "Miss Thistlebottom" standing adversarially at the front of a classroom, conjugating verbs at the blackboard, yardstick menacingly in hand, ready to crack it summarily over a distracted skull. (If you attended a Catholic school, as I did, you can readily conjure up "Attila the Nun.")

So fear not. I promise to make the excursion through these pages enjoyable, memorable and, where appropriate, humorous. At the same time, I know you expect hard-hitting information you can apply immediately, and not just theoretical language discussions which must simmer on a back burner for some time before they can be ingested. Let's begin, then. Let's take a closer look at principles of language skill development that they don't teach us in school. And let's keep in the forefront of our awareness the attitude that among the lessons most truly worth knowing in life are those we teach ourselves.

Tom Stapleton
Glendale, California
1994

"Whether you think you can or think you can't, you're right."
– Henry Ford

Overview

This chapter presents a digest of the rest of the book and begins charting a course for you to follow in developing a procedure for getting your thoughts across to readers or listeners. To do your job proficiently, you need to know how to best organize, compose, and deliver messages. Critical in developing a base of knowledge on which you build is your attitude. Believe in yourself, believe you *can* accomplish, and you'll succeed. That isn't just a platitude, either.

As Jesse Jackson has told us, with the right attitude, we can increase our aptitude; with confidence, we increase our competence. But we need a *strategy* for accomplishment.

Numbers Count

How do we begin strategizing? By assessing how our efforts are now directed. Time–management specialists tell us that we spend about one or two days a week at work writing and speaking. That's up to about 40% of our time on the job, leaving only about three days to do all the things our job description says we were hired to do. No wonder we feel overloaded. It's no surprise that our message sending suffers as a result.

In business communications, many of us needlessly inflate the English language and end up confusing or boring the audience. Look over this statement which ended a memo written by a bank vice president:

> *"It does not appear that there would be any need for us to continue ownership of this stock."*

In this example, isn't the writer merely saying, "*We do not need this stock anymore*"? Of course! Why, then, didn't the VP use just seven words to convey a message that took eighteen? Is it possible that a direct, simple, uncluttered statement violates some "law" that says, "Where ten words will say the same as two, use ten"? Are we conditioned to think that our writing, in particular, is judged by the pound?

Learning to Streamline

Most of us, whether in our written business communications or in speeches we prepare, tend to add unnecessary wording. The result is that we often contradict the way we are in person by the way we come across on paper or at the podium. All too often our letters, memos, reports, briefings, or presentations are impersonal and mechanical— displaying a stiff, sterile tone devoid of human contact. Take, as another instance, this statement from a talk given by a data processing chief:

> *"Since the program began, it has become apparent*
> *that participation in the program is not*
> *economically feasible due to the low percentage*
> *of approval that has been realized on these applications."*

What he meant was, *"This program is not paying off for us because we approve so few applications."* Fourteen words replace thirty-one. Imagine how many thousands of words people with whom you communicate read or listen to every day. What's going to make the few you write or speak stand out? For one thing, conciseness.

But, of course, communicating successfully is not merely a numbers game. It also has to do with organization and appropriate language choice, the twin pillars of forceful, dynamic message sending.

Ten Simple Steps

The entire contents of this book can be distilled into ten relatively simple steps to follow in strategically preparing an oral or written communication. Each step is covered in one or more chapters. Certainly, you'll find many more than ten steps delineated throughout. But for now, let's go over these steps which are really comprehensive systems or processes. Think of what I discuss as preliminary information. Together, we're going to begin putting together a blueprint, so to speak, or a frame of reference from which we'll build.

Don't be concerned that you're not yet getting all the information you'll need to learn how to communicate more effectively.

We're still at the overview stage; I'll be fleshing out the concepts as we proceed.

Incidentally, the same steps apply whether your final product is an oral or written message. You'll normally prepare at least a written draft of a speech, so bringing all the principles in this book full circle means you'll be ready no matter what the nature of your communication. Where it's necessary to do certain things differently when composing an oral presentation, I'll discuss specific differences.

Step 1 – Collect Your Thoughts

For openers, it's important to begin concentrating on the task at hand. You're attempting to focus your attention on the message and start formulating its various aspects. I'll discuss how to assess whether your communication is primarily **Action, Information only**, or a combination of both. Know your objective in the first place for sending your message and then *outline* its main points, if only mentally. No matter how rushed you are, such preparation is time well spent. The payoff comes when your audience understands your message and responds favorably.

Step 2 – Profile Your Audience

Other human beings, sharing much in common with you, read or listen to your messages. Keep in mind that they will react not only to what you write or say but to *how* you come across, picking up images and impressions you convey. Ask yourself how much the audience already knows about your subject, what their experience is in relation to it, and how you can best motivate them. I'll give you suggestions on asking a series of questions to get at who makes up your audience and how they're likely to react.

Step 3 – Converse With Your Audience

Imagine you're communicating one-to-one with your readers or listeners. A written document is read by only one given person at a time anyway, and a group of listeners is comprised of individual men and women. Communicate with them personally, intimately. You do that by the way you speak, and by speaking from the heart.

Ask yourself as you prepare to write, "How would I say this to someone across the desk from me, or over the phone?" Everyday language is what people are accustomed to hearing and what they use when they speak. So don't jar the "mind's ear" with business bafflegab. I'll show you ways of revising your style to incorporate audience considerations.

Step 4 – Choose Your Tone

Consider what attitude you want to take in your message — firm, friendly, humorous, apologetic, and the like. Once you decide, stick to it, otherwise you'll only confuse your audience. To illustrate why consistent tone is important: a collection agency letter began by telling the reader about his arrears account, leading up to the statement, "You leave us no recourse but to take appropriate legal action." The writer then shifted gears and concluded the letter by saying, "Please call us about making arrangements to grant an extension." Just *what* stand was the writer taking? You'll learn more about what *Tone* is and how to control it as we continue.

Step 5 – Decide Which Type of Opening is Appropriate

People neither read nor listen to your messages with the same effort or concern you put into preparing them. An **Emphatic** *Opening* approach attempts to get the audience's attention immediately and hold it, to make your communication (whether to a customer or a co-worker) stand out. On the other hand, a less attention-getting *Opening*, known as **Low-key**, may be preferable. I'll discuss when to make the choice, and how to control the application.

Step 6 – Use "Message Mechanics" to Manage the Communication

Short sentences, active voice, concise paragraphs — each helps you communicate more effectively and is known as a mechanical element. You can create lasting visual images by understanding how to integrate these elements of style into your messages. This step will take up a significant portion of topic discussion. It's important to be careful of using jargon (which simply means specialized language), especially when talking or speaking to the uninitiated. If a technical term is necessary, explain what it means.

Step 7 – Don't Sag in the Middle

The middle of the message is what's contained in the *Body*. Again, organization is the key. **Content Mapping** techniques will help streamline the communication — for you and your audience. They'll complement my presentation of Message Mechanics.

Step 8 – Add Incentive

Convey audience benefits. Readers and listeners naturally want to know what good your message will do them. Let them know what the payback is for attending to your message by spelling it out. Maybe you can point out a way to save time or money, to put human resources to better use, or to reach a decision. If you think about it, aren't your business communications really tools to facilitate effective decision making? Persuading or convincing others means being able to sell your points. I'll devote considerable explanation and examples to this subject.

Step 9 – Decide How to Close Your Message

Use the *Closing* to reinforce your objective. Don't just run out of ideas and stop or, nearly as inefficient, begin unnecessarily repeating yourself. We often water down our closing comments because we don't think about summing up. Your audience can't divine what you intend; tell them. They shouldn't have to play Sherlock Holmes in trying to deduce the "mystery" of your message. It should be elementary. A closing in a letter such as "Let's meet to discuss this further" merely drifts off. In fact, such a vague and uncertain statement may detract from the valuable information that precedes it.

People tend to remember first what they read last. You'll find three proven *Closing* categories analyzed in this book, with instructions on how to apply them in varying situations.

Step 10 – Review Your Messages Regularly

I'll give you suggestions on how to evaluate your efforts, to help you develop communication models and do better with succeeding messages. You'll be assessing honestly whether you've gone through each of the preceding steps in developing your communications so you can learn to do better next time.

Wide Range of Application

My intent is to give you assistance with any type of message you have responsibility for generating or reviewing: technical/non-technical, formal/informal, internal/external. It matters not whether you're preparing letters, memos, reports, studies, proposals, briefings, meetings, user manuals, procedures documents, performance evaluations, E-mail, management presentations, customer orientations, or a note to the milkman. We're going to look at the similarities, rather than the dissimilarities, of business communications.

And a by-product of that observation process is that you'll gain first-time or supplemental knowledge, knowledge that will prepare you confidently for viewing any communications task as an opportunity to demonstrate how professional you are.

Remember that very few people reach the top without first cultivating useful communication skills.   So before taking pen in hand or taking the podium . . . first, take care.

Overcoming "Page Fright"

Taking care begins with a series of pre-composition steps common to any communication task.   Most of us are faced with what I call the "page-fright" response (when you're speaking, of course, the symptom is stage fright).   You know the feeling: there you sit, a blank sheet of paper or word processing screen in front of you, your mind a jumble, your throat dry, your palms beginning to sweat. You fidget, stall, procrastinate.   There's a vague feeling that you do know something about what you want to write or say, you just don't have the foggiest notion of how to go about it.

And it's not like you haven't done this before. You have. But you doubt it was your best effort. And now you have to do it again. But it doesn't get any easier. Why must you go through this agony of reinventing the wheel every time? *How come* they don't teach us this in school?

What you're faced with, quite simply, is the responsibility for making order out of chaos. You'll find a most efficient application of your time and effort by breaking down what may seem like an overwhelming task into a series of smaller, more manageable tasks. This approach basically involves thinking in terms of the "lowest common denominator." What level can you reduce your labor to?

At the outset, try to condition yourself not to think in terms of the final product. That will come as the result of a series of adeptly handled processes. As Peters and Waterman remind us in *The Pursuit of Excellence*, effective task accomplishment rests not so much on doing any one thing 1000% better, rather on doing a thousand things 1% better. Admittedly, you're faced with the prospect of having to do a "thousand things" (it only *seems* like that many!) when you set out to prepare an oral or written communication. But the key understanding at this point is that you are, in fact, preparing. You're not yet doing.

Devising Your Game Plan

So the primary pre–composition step is to devise a game plan. No sports team would take the field or court without first putting together a game plan, one which strategically emphasizes their strong points, plays to the opponents' weaknesses, and incorporates an optimistic design for an advantageous outcome — in short, one which stresses *winning*. How do you successfully do that when the playing field is life or business and the stakes are not just victory but survival? How do you play to win and not just to *not lose*?

The adage that "long after the score is forgotten we remember the game" comes to mind. The game analogy is apt, because that's what communications are all about. They're a game. And, like all games, successfully communicating is governed by certain sets of rules, although I prefer the term *guidelines*, because the idea of rules connotes something inflexible, chiseled in stone.

Let's think, then, in terms of guidelines. That's what we're now going to begin examining in detail, to help make more informed choices about the processes necessary to achieve the desired outcome, to get results . . . to win. Look at this diagram:

ACTION ◄─► INFO ONLY

1) Organize MESSAGE:
   5 Steps

2) Profile AUDIENCE:
   (Self-Interests)
   5 Questions

3) Think STRUCTURE:
   4 Elements

Planning your communication incorporates how to best organize, to marshal your efforts so that "economy of motion" is evident. We want to accomplish maximum results with a minimum of effort, to work smarter, not harder.   The information in the preceeding diagram contains the building blocks of effective communications. They're each part of the plan.

I'll go through them completely and comprehensively with you, supplementing my discussion with examples, and giving you an opportunity to interact with this book through occasional exercises (not tests; they're too academic!). This way you can incrementally measure your progress as we proceed.

Not Just An Old Bromide

The key to improving communication skills in the planning process is to become aware of strength and weakness patterns in the way you write and speak. Then, you learn to monitor choices for making your message sending more productive. The mortar that holds these building blocks together is *practice*. The right practice makes perfect, as our grade-school teachers constantly reminded us. They also taught us that we learn by doing.

I encourage you to participate with me by taking advantage of the opportunity to complete the exercises I mentioned. You can work at your own pace, and no one is going to grade you or report your results to anyone else. So "achievement stress" is eliminated right away.

We're all creatures of habit. Recognizing the broad patterns of behavior that mark our personalities and actions is a useful way to control that behavior, to bend it more to our own ends. The data in the diagram on page 8 helps us in that analysis. I identify as a jumping-off point two categories or classifications of messages: Action and Info only.

Any oral or written communication can be readily slotted as one or the other, and sometimes as both. The double-headed arrow between the words at the top of the diagram indicates that some "back & forth" may occur. For example, any action message contains information. And you may prepare a communication this month which you intend as information only, but which spurs action next month. The point is that these are not mutually exclusive categories.

Varieties of Messages

Now, think for a moment about patterns apparent in your own written documents or oral messages. Do you tend to generate one type more than the other? Are your communications a mix of the two? Here are some examples of Action messages:

* Recommendation   * Motivational talk
   report   * Order memo
* Sales letter   * Your résumé

In short, any time you're trying to persuade or convince — to change behavior — your communication is an Action message. It may reflect a situation as routine as directing a vendor to re-supply or as consequential as seeking approval to make a multi-million dollar purchase.

<u>Information only</u> messages might be any of these:

* Cancellation notice   * Management briefing
* Status report   * After-dinner speech

This category applies primarily to communications whose intent is to educate. But when you write an <u>Action</u> message, you don't stop there; you're also trying to get someone to begin (or stop) doing something, or continue what he/she/they have already been doing.

Communication Categories

You'll note that under each of the category designations in the diagram on page 8 a geometric configuration appears. <u>Action</u> messages are circular. The sender comes back around a full 360 degrees to generate a whole, satisfyingly complete message which "rounds out" understanding.

An <u>Information only</u> message, on the other hand, is linear: it presents data straightforwardly, in 1-2-3 or A-B-C fashion. This isn't to imply that an <u>Information only</u> message can't also be complete, but that its method of idea presentation differs slightly. There isn't necessarily a need to come back around full circle.

Typically, an <u>Action</u> message doubles back in the *Closing* on a point or points made earlier, either from the *Opening* or the *Body*, deliberately reinforcing to drive home the importance of the communication. An <u>Information only</u> message may reinforce, too, but so close an alignment between the closing and earlier portions of what's being communicated usually isn't necessary. We'll observe the differences at greater length when we begin looking at sample communications.

Gray Matter Matters

Some of you may be verbally oriented, whereas others among you may be more mathematically oriented. Those in the former category may respond more directly to the terms <u>Action</u> and <u>Information only</u>. For those in the latter, the circle and line (geometric configurations) on page 8 may have more significant effect. It's been said that the two basic types of human personalities are verbal and mathematic. Verbally oriented people go into such professions as writing, acting, public relations, and so forth. The mathematically oriented among us gravitate toward accounting, medicine, the sciences — by and large, technical professions. Right-brained and left-brained is another way of relating to verbal versus mathematical designations. Rules of math are exact and consistent (2+2 always = 4). Not so with language, where it seems exceptions $\geq$ rules.

> [Obiter dicta: In some cognitive-psychology circles,
> the "whole brain" label is finding renewed favor.
> Maybe a greater truism about human personalities
> is that the two kinds of people in the world are
> those who divide others into two categories,
> and those who don't!]

Systematic Approach

Once you've decided which of the two categories applies to your message, you're ready to begin going through three systems or processes designed to guide you through the pre-composition portion of preparing any message. I call this systematic approach a *work plan*. The best way to make use of such a plan is to understand it thoroughly and use it consistently. It will then help make your communication tasks manageable and aid in guiding your progress as you incrementally fulfill responsibilities.

Step–By–Step

Remember that, at this juncture, we're concerned only with processes to complete, a little at a time. We're laying a foundation upon which we'll build, gradually shifting from process to product. You may find that you already go through a similar system in the way you now prepare your messages. But you may not be as consistent or as thorough as this work plan can help you to be.

Will you have to go through all the processes each time you generate a communication? For a while, yes. But the more familiar you become with the work plan, the sooner you'll assimilate it, and the more it will become automatic for you. The learning curve isn't very steep, but your ascent will be well worth it. (Think of it as rising to new heights!)

```
The First Process:
Organize MESSAGE
```

        The diagram on page 8 shows this process comprising 5 steps. Taken as a whole, they're designed to help you collect your thoughts. Many messages fail because of lack of organization. The steps discussed here give you an opportunity to develop an understanding of just what you want to convey, and then to devise a "blueprint" of that message.

        Incidentally, the steps flow in a deductive fashion; that is, they proceed from the general to the particular. Deductive thinking helps you corral the thoughts in your head, which don't exist in any particular order (except maybe random!). They're there, all right, but it's your responsibility to dig them out and call them up.   I'll talk more about deductive reasoning later in Chapter 4 when discussing paragraphs and idea flow. Here, then, are the steps:

Step #1 – Define Your Objective

        This is your purpose for message sending, the reason you identify for communicating with your audience in the first place. It's important to determine the broad subject matter about which you intend to educate the reader. Link your objective with whether the message will be Action or Info only. And don't worry when starting out that you may not have any more than a preliminary idea of what you want to say or write. It's perfectly understandable if, at this early stage, your objective isn't completely formulated.   You'll be fleshing it out, shaping and refining it as you go along.

Stone Soup

        Let's say, for example, that you're preparing a memo to your boss on the subject of the IBM Personal System 2 computer.   Maybe you're not even sure whether the memo is to be <u>Action</u> or <u>Info only</u>. For now, your objective is merely to discuss the IBM computer.   Fine. At least you've taken the first step in making what's known as *stone soup*. A bit of a digression is apropos here:

> In medieval times, a group of hungry serfs got
> together to plan a meal. But provisions were in
> drastically short supply, and none of the
> serfs had any idea what to prepare. All
> were agreed that it was mealtime, but
> what would be the substance to dine on?
> After a round of futile arguing, one of the
> serfs said, "Look, let's just start with *something*.
> Here, I've got this stone. What does anyone else
> have to throw in the pot?"

> The others looked at him as though he'd been out
> in the open sward too long, but they slowly got the
> idea. At least they'd stopped arguing and were
> starting to plan anything for the meal,
> out of which they hoped something would
> come to eat.

> So, a second serf said, "I have this grass,"
> and a third chimed in, "Here's a bucket
> of water." The others, in turn, soon came
> up with roots, berries — you get the
> idea. Eventually, they had the ingredients for
> a soup, and could throw away the stone.

The moral of the fable is, when encountering the "page fright" syndrome I spoke about earlier, you can stop the futile wheelspinning by contriving *anything* to give you a push. You can abandon it later — throw away the stone, so to speak — and feel confident that you are, at the very least, underway in message sending.   You can always return to this step once you're a little farther along to get a firmer grasp on your objective.   Ultimately, if you don't have that grasp, can you expect your readers or listeners to?

Is This Trip Necessary?

You may even find, when determining your objective, that a written message isn't at all necessary. Maybe a memo isn't called for, rather a meeting or a phone call will do it. If, for instance, you were a supervisor terminating a subordinate's employment (firing someone) you wouldn't inform the employee in a memo. You'd have a one-to-one in your office.

Let's keep in mind the sample suggestion that, in preparing this memo, the objective is to discuss the IBM Personal System 2. We'll use it as a continuing example.

Step #2 – Outline Your Points

Sketch out a flow of related topics pertinent to your subject matter. Some research may be required at this stage. You're trying to determine what you want to say about the IBM computer. What do you already know? Do you have the facts right? What further information do you need to obtain? Over the years of conducting my communications workshops, I've become a stickler for outlines. I can usually spot a message a mile away that hasn't been outlined. Its underpinnings are shaky.

Your outline doesn't have to resemble one of those cumbersome formats your seventh-grade English teacher made you adhere to for book reports. Remember those levels of indentation indicated by Roman numerals, then capital letters, followed by Arabic numbering, and all that rigmarole? I don't want to offend any of you who may have been quite happily using such an outlining system since junior high school. If it works for you, who am I to quibble? But if you'd like to streamline your efforts, I'll give you three suggested ways of effectively outlining:

■ Ask yourself a series of questions.

   a. What's the best order of presentation for my message as a whole? (Normally, begin with a purpose statement, then recommendations or a summary of key points. Go on to necessary background, discussion, and additional details.)

b. What's the best psychological order
of ideas for factual discussion? (Consider
importance or significance, size, geographical
location, alphabetical sequence.)

c. Does the audience need to compare one set
of facts with another or others? (Think of
how to present facts for easiest comparison.)

d. Is it important that the audience follow my
thinking process? (If so, consider how best to
concisely present facts. Conciseness of
expression is discussed in Chapters 3 and 4.)

e. Can some information be understood
more quickly and easily if it's presented in
a table, chart, or graph? (Visual aides can
enhance your point presentation.)

■ <u>Use the Wheel-&-Spoke Outline.</u> Also known as a
"brainstorming" outline, this is a particularly helpful
process of keeping ideas from falling through the cracks by
doing a little conceptual blockbusting. Its greatest benefit
is helping you break through to your message. Since we're
using the IBM computer example as our model, first draw a
wheel (or circle) and write "IBM P/S 2" inside it, as the
diagram below depicts. Now we add spokes to represent
points. We'll talk about "cost," "software," and "training,"
for instance. Already we've got a skeleton. Of course, we
have to put meat on the bones. But we're still in the pre-
composition phase. So the detail that we're going to write or
talk about will come later.

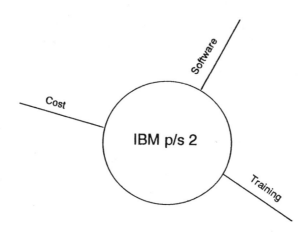

This is starting to lean toward becoming an <u>Action</u> message.

The wheel-&-spoke outline can lift your thinking out of the doldrums, getting you on course and in motion with your message. Plus, its design allows for flexibility. By nature, the structure is organic; you can add to it or subtract from it as you polish your preparation. I'll show you how shortly when we return to it.

■ <u>Follow the "Management Report" flow.</u>   You proceed as shown:

          * Executive Summary
          * Purpose
          * Background
          * Discussion
          * Justification
          * Recommendation

The primary application for this is both oral and written reports. I'm not implying that your final message will necessarily contain only those six segments in the above order. The segments and the order are for your *outline*. You can modify and rearrange as necessary.

Different Strokes

As I've mentioned, I always suggest outlining all messages. But don't think it has to be a formal process. Sometimes all that's required is a mental outline, especially for brief, routine letters or memos. You may only need to think through a couple of points to make before dictating or composing the message. Still another method that works well is using 3" X 5" index cards on which you jot down thoughts. Then you group the cards accordingly (such as the categories suggested by the "Management Report" flow on page 16). This system allows for idea shuffling to assist you in coming up with the most direct alignment of points presented in logical order.

A final note on outlines: A well-constructed outline serves as a table of contents, so you're conserving time and effort. The process of outlining can also be thought of as a "frontloading" formula. This means you spend more time preparing the message and less actually having to compose it. It's like building an early-innings lead in a baseball game so you don't have to worry about playing catch-up later. The lesson is, when you stay on top of things they don't get out from under you. Never have truer words been written when applied to outlines. So make it a habit . . . and remember, all habits are hard to break, even the good ones.

Step #3 – Give the Benefits of Your Message

Let's return to the wheel-&-spoke outline and the management report flow (pages 15 and 16). We're going to add a justification spoke to our IBM computer subject, but we're going to label it "Benefits." Ask yourself what the value is to the audience of your message. How will the information explain important data? What's at stake for the reader? What's the payback? Benefits are selling points which help to motivate and persuade your audience, especially important if you're preparing an <u>Action</u> message. We've already determined that the subject matter for our sample message was leaning in this direction. Now we're going to pin it down.

Push the *Positive* Button

The general rule of thumb in the pre-composition stage is that if you don't have benefits to convey to your audience, you're not readying an <u>Action</u> message. Yet every time you generate a communication designed to get action, you are attempting to *sell* your ideas, to win over your audience. It's not always an easy task, but it can be accomplished by accentuating the positive.

Think of times you've been in the market to buy — whether a house, a car, a new stereo, for instance. Do you remember the sales person? Was high pressure applied? Did anything put you off about the transaction? What factored into your decision to buy, or not to buy? Given that the price is right and that you feel you're getting a good deal, you'll make the buy, very often *regardless of whether you think you need or want the object of purchase.*

Understanding Needs

Why so? Are we that easily manipulated? (Granted, some of us are!) Psychologists tell us that buying can be predicated on want or need, sometimes on both. But what's most important to understand now is that — when we're in the market — we buy largely because we feel the seller understands us; i.e., understands our wants or needs. Your job, to be a successful communicator, is to tap into the audience's wants or needs and satisfy them.

Here's a good example of what I'm talking about:

Say you're going to drive from New York to San Francisco. You *need* transportation. It can be had by way of a '63 Chevy wagon. But suppose you had the opportunity to make the trip in a spanking new Ferrari Testarossa? Which vehicle would you *want*? (I know what you're thinking: the Chevy would be less likely, as you nudge up against speed limits, to draw the attention of highway patrols!) Given that all other factors are equal, though — and that you could afford the exorbitant price tag and insurance — you'll most likely opt for the Ferrari. Why not? After all, we're only fantasizing here anyway, right? Isn't it easy to imagine yourself behind the wheel right now, flying low over Iowa? Which is another way of asking, Isn't it easy to get caught up in the fun, the emotion, of what we're imagining?

Emotional Appeal

Much of what we buy, or buy into, is a function of emotion. And that's what's important to know when you're trying to *sell.* It's easy to imagine the advantages of driving cross-country in a Ferrari compared with an antique Chevy. (Doesn't the fantasy just tie up your adrenal glands with your heartstrings?) Successful salespeople know how to appeal to the emotions.   And we tend to warm up to somebody who seems to understand us. We all love to be sold. No one loves to be backed into a corner, though. (Can you conjure up an image of a high-pressure door-to-door salesman, trying to sell you a suit?)

[**Obiter dicta:** A few years ago, an article in the Harvard Business Review featured a purveyor of corporate jets. To close sales, he took prospective buyers on a breathtaking flight. What he was selling was the *excitement* as much as the jet itself.]

Ours is a market-driven economy, and buy/sell transactions are constantly occurring, in business and life in general. Every time you attempt to persuade or motivate, you're attempting to sell your point of view, to get the person(s) on the other end to buy in. So, then, when preparing an <u>Action</u> message, let's dig a little first to determine its value for the audience. Here's where we add a fourth spoke to the outline wheel, as this diagram shows:

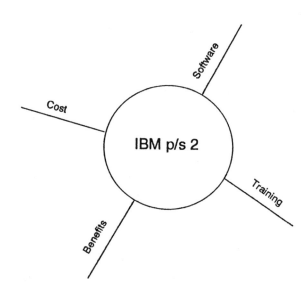

The new spoke is *Benefits*, conveying necessary justification info for your audience. Here's a thinking prompt for you: when trying to come up with benefits, maybe you'll be pointing out in your message a way that the IBM P/S 2 can save time or money, or perhaps boost productivity by putting people to better use, or even help the reader — your boss — to reach a decision. (I'm referring here to one of the ten simple steps from earlier in this chapter, step 8, page 5.) Certainly, you can have more, or fewer, than just these three branches. But it's always helpful to realize that you're normally trying to get your audiences to make at least two decisions when you send messages:

To decide that your communication is worth reading or listening to, and that your communication is worth going along with; i.e., buying into.

You make your message a tool for effective decision making to occur by incorporating benefits. Later, in Chapter 4, I'll talk about locating benefits in the *Body* for maximum impact.

Step #4 – Make Your Message Interesting

What have you read or listened to recently that was of interest to you, and why was it so? Think of novels, TV shows, magazine articles, presentations that you've found compelling. Haven't there been times when you've wished you could write that way or captivate an audience in similar spellbinding fashion? Well, maybe you'll never have to write with Pulitzer Prize–winning ability, nor deliver a sermon on the mount. But every day of your life you communicate. Some of the contexts are routine, while others are much more weighty. The messages that stick with us and others, though — the ones that are most memorable — are invariably those that are most interesting.

Interest Injectors

The question is begged, then: How do we make our messages interesting? Professional writers and speakers use many tools of the trade to maintain reader or listener interest, keeping their messages forceful and dynamic, driving their points home. It's really all in the technique. You don't need inborn writing or speaking ability to learn how to sustain interest in your message sending. Remember one of the main themes of this book: skills can be developed and sharpened to help you meet any communications challenge with confidence and know–how.

In Chapter 3, when I talk about ingredients affecting the tone of messages, also known as the mechanical elements of language, I'll amplify discussion of how to interject interest. But to give you something to think about at this point, begin retraining yourself to eliminate long, dense paragraphs in your writing. When you speak, concentrate on keeping the message as simple and direct as possible, thereby increasing the likelihood that your listeners will find what you're saying of interest.

Self–Check

It's important to supplement what you're learning in this book with healthy amounts of self-analysis. Take some time before proceeding much further to look over copies of documents you've written recently. Examine drafts or notes of oral presentations you've delivered. Are they interesting? Making a message interesting is critical in selling your ideas, so I'll devote a considerable portion of the text to this concern.

Funny You Should Mention That

You might ask yourself how effective, and how *appropriate*, humor is in adding interest to a business message. Granted, formal technical documents, written for a readership you're not greatly familiar with, probably don't call for humor. It seems, though, that humor is more allowable in an oral rather than a written communications context. We're more likely to hear evidence of its use than we are to read it. Why so?

My theory is that you can better gauge your audience when they're right in front of you, that there's a two-way stream of thought occurring. You get immediate feedback. You can read your listeners' body language — whether they're maintaining eye contact, yawning distractedly, or dozing off: all telltale signs about the "boredom level" of your message. And, of course, you can make immediate adjustments. (If your jokes are bombing, get serious.)

It's not easy to make similar determinations when you write. What I call a "lag factor" can work against you. By that I mean, what's funny to you on Tuesday morning when you're writing a letter might not be so comedic to the reader on Friday afternoon. And humor is typically a slippery, personal concept anyway.

Saving Grace

But humor can have beneficial effects. I've seen many a dull, dry document punched up with just a little application of wit on the part of the writer, as I've heard many a dry-subject talk salvaged by a judicious sprinkling of humor throughout. Humor can help to anchor your ideas in the audience's memory, underscoring and lending more impact to them.

It's disheartening to see that, over the past few years, we've gotten to the point in corporate America that we take ourselves dead serious on the job, as though the subject matter of our oral and written communications were of life–and–death import. It isn't. We need to learn to relax a bit and deal with one another on a human, humane level. Humor is a valuable tool in achieving this end.

Winning Over the Audience

I'm not advocating that we become "sit–down comedians" each time we prepare a message. Besides, that's much easier said than done. (Just try coming up with some original, laughingly funny lines.) Nor am I suggesting that cracking jokes in our communications will in itself make our messages memorable. Humor is no substitute for lack of preparation or substance. But it can defuse skepticism, getting the audience in your corner so they'll be more likely to hear you out, and go along.

Two examples here will serve as a wrap–up. The first is about a friend of mine at a technical consulting group in Colorado Springs. The firm does much specialty work with the Department of Defense, and in the process submits many government proposals (a type of document, by the way, tailor–made to benefit from the capabilities of desktop publishing, if ever there was one). My friend's idea is to one day compose a proposal entirely in cartoon motif, complete with genre drawings and dialogue bubbles. I know he's reacting against the typically stilted style of proposals so long mandated by the government. Alas, I fear his brave and long–overdue suggestion is doomed not likely to see the light of day — at least not until radical changes are made regarding governmental expectations that proposals be written in "bureaucratese."

The second example is about another friend at a bank in Los Angeles who submits quarterly feasibility studies to upper management. He recently wrote about the effects of weather on bank real–estate transactions, lacing his narrative with hilarious personifications of natural elements such as Snow, Heat, Occluded Fronts, and the like. I know you don't have the benefit of seeing the original, so you have to trust me. It was funny. Not only to me, but to upper management, where things really count. In fact, their reaction was that the study, compared with other similar dry discussions, read like a breath of fresh air.

Proceed With Caution

If you're ever in doubt about whether to use humor, ask yourself, "Could this be a career–limiting move on my part?" Remember that a little risktaking is sometimes necessary to achieve desired goals. But always take calculated risks, unless, that is, you're the type who thrills in throwing caution to the wind. Let's say, for now, that in the IBM P/S 2 memo we're preparing, humor is inappropriate. But we do want to make the message interesting. We'll analyze how very shortly.

Step #5 – Decide What Reaction You Want

You always want some kind of reaction, or you wouldn't be message sending in the first place. Keep in mind that your decision must be specific. What, if anything, do you want the audience members to do? This step is a spinoff of step one; very often your *objective* is linked with your desired *reaction*. Here's where we bring deductive reasoning to completion. We're at the point of having to make up our minds whether the memo we're going to compose will be <u>Action</u> or <u>Info only</u>. Let's review the two categories again for a moment.

<u>Action</u> messages require a twofold reaction: we want the audience to understand, and then to do something. <u>Info only</u> messages require simply that the message be understood. We're writing about the IBM P/S 2, and we're leaning toward the action category. Knowing what reaction we want will help us cap the process.

Back to the Work Plan

Suppose we want our boss's approval to purchase a fleet of computers for the department. Now we know we have an <u>Action</u> document. So we're trying to get the boss to spend a good bit of money. We'd better make sure we're *selling*, pointing out benefits. Where will we make the request in the memo itself? The opening? The closing? The answer will depend on the strategy we're developing based on our work plan. In fact, we may decide that the best course of action is not even to make a request for approval to purchase the IBM P/S 2.

Here's why.   Sometimes, we unwittingly usurp our bosses' decision-making responsibility by, in effect, making up their minds for them. Psychologists tell us that, generally, people prefer being presented with all the facts — being led to the brink of a decision — and then deciding for themselves.

A highly effective strategy, then, is to co-opt the boss into the decision-making process. (Remember one of the branches on the wheel-&-spoke outline on page 16 under <u>Benefits</u>: helping the reader reach a decision.) A better plan might be to ask the reader to attend an upcoming IBM computer exhibit locally (unless there's one in Hawaii!), where the virtues of the hardware and software will extol themselves. Granted, this type of suggestion is an interim step in getting our boss to approve making the buy.   But that may be preferable to coming out point blank and making a recommendation.

Your audience profile, though, may indicate that just such a direct recommendation is called for. Let's move on to this second system in the work plan, to determine more about your audience and what will motivate readers or listeners.

Chapter 1 Review

Here are the significant points presented in this chapter:

    ☞ Develop and stick to your *work plan* as a
        pre-composition process.

    ☞ Organize your message before writing by:
         - defining your objective
         - outlining
         - giving benefits
         - adding interest
         - deciding on the desired reaction

*"Do you expect the greatest of arts to
be acquired by slight endeavors?"*
– Epictetus, 2nd Century

Overview

This chapter details the process of profiling your audience (readers, for written messages; listeners, for spoken). It explains a systematic attempt to focus your communication, to target it for specifically intended people. Getting a composite idea of who your audience is and how its members are likely to react to your message complements the organizational steps just discussed in Chapter 1. Assessing your audience takes some effort, but the outcome — getting *results* — is well worth it.

```
The Second Process:
Profile AUDIENCE
```

You're now ready to deal with the human element in message sending, putting your best foot forward in demonstrating that your communication addresses the self-interests of the audience members.

Behavior Based on Self-Interests

Why is it important to keep in mind people's self-interests when we're preparing a written or oral document? Another lesson in human psychology is again appropriate to demonstrate.

Behaviorists tell us that all people act in terms of what satisfies self-interests; doing so is a normal, healthy trait. It's difficult for us to do anything that contradicts those ends. To illustrate: If you hold your finger over a fire, you won't leave it there for long. Our involuntary reaction towards self-preservation causes us to pull away when the heat becomes too intense. Acting in our own self-interests is what moderates our risktaking tendencies. It's what causes us to look both ways before crossing the street.

Many times, in proposal development workshops I've conducted, I've tried to drive home the idea that, for instance, the most important section of a proposal volume to a facilities planner will be the section titled "Facilities." That person probably won't read much else of the proposal, except for the executive summary, if that. Isn't it obvious where this reader's interests will lie?

Doing For Others . . . and Ourselves

Even selfless, altruistic actions are generated, at least in part, by our own interests. I have a friend who volunteers much of her time to tutor disadvantaged children. She works wonders with these unfortunate kids, bestowing on them much love and concern. She's a considerate, giving person able to accomplish what she does because of the fact that she can live outside herself and do for others. But, at the same time, she's doing for herself. On many occasions she's related to me the deep sense of satisfaction she feels as a result of her volunteer efforts. In fact, for her, that sense of satisfaction and accomplishment makes it all worthwhile.

The old adage "'Tis better to give than receive" rings true in her case, and in the case of any of us who gain a positive inner feeling when doing good for others. My point is that there are two beneficiaries: those we help . . . and ourselves.

And there's absolutely nothing wrong with this. We can't help but behave in terms of satisfying our own self-interests. Much of the good done in the world is predicated on this psychological reality. When you're preparing a communication, your task is to demonstrate that your self-interests *and those of your audience* mesh. How do you do this? By asking — and doing your best to answer — the series of questions that starts on page 30, trying to flesh out your understanding of how best to incorporate your readers' or listeners' point of view in what you have to convey.

A note of caution before we proceed: We're about to embark on a less-than-scientific process because human beings are never 100% safely predictable. What works for you on one occasion with a specific audience might not work on another with the same people.

Profiling In Layers

For purposes of economy, I use a singular reference when discussing the audience makeup — "reader" or "listener." Of course, the political reality is that you often communicate with multiple audience members. Typically, when writing messages, we must profile not only the ultimate reader or readers, but reviewers (who may be bosses or co-workers), people to whom we send courtesy copies, and even hidden readers of whom we're completely unaware but who just may have decision-making responsibility regarding our subject matter.

What are we to do, then? We can't possibly anticipate or take into account everybody who might receive our messages, can we?

No. So the best course of action is to try to identify a composite type of audience member or primary type of person you're likely to be communicating with. For example, a number of years ago I wrote an article that was published in *Ladies Home Journal* magazine [see pages 145 and 146]. Hundreds of thousands of people probably read the piece. How did I profile so many diverse readers?

As part of their writers' guidelines, the magazine editors sent me a composite description of their typical reader:

— a woman, between the ages of 18 and 44
— more likely to be college-educated than women
   of her mother's generation
— getting married later in life and having
   fewer children than previous generations of women
— more likely to be concerned with subject matter
   having to do with career considerations (such
   as competing with and succeeding against men)
   than with stretching the homemaker's budget

Not so diverse a group after all. The image I had in mind as I wrote helped me focus on a reader I could directly address. Like my wife, who fits the profile of a typical *Ladies Home Journal* reader.

Common Ground

So when it comes to readers or listeners, don't worry about numbers. It doesn't matter whether your audience is comprised of one person or a hundred thousand people. Concentrate on what those human beings (who are very much like you, incidentally) have in common with one another and with you, and then establish common ground for communicating. Granted, the fewer the number of people you're sending a message to, and the better you know them, the easier it is to complete a profile.

But don't fall into the trap of trying to be all things to all men. You can't possibly succeed. There's an old Irish saying that, "If you try to please everybody, nobody will like it." Strive to generate a message that any reader or listener would be happy to claim as his or her own.

Let's focus on the similarities of behavioral traits, rather than the dissimilarities, among ourselves and our audience members when we write or speak. That way, the profiling process becomes less intimidating and inhibiting and a "free flow" of effective communication can occur. Here are five questions to ask:

Question #1 – Who Are my Audience Members?

You're trying to determine at this stage the titles or positions of the people who'll receive your message. It's often helpful, in a business setting, to pin down whether they are superiors, peers, or subordinates. For example, in the hypothetical IBM computer memo, you're writing to someone up the chain of command, to a person with decision-making authority. Let's dig a little deeper and find out about his or her *responsibility.* Let's say you're an accountant and your boss's title is Accounting Department Manager. Where do that person's self-interests lie? What should you be emphasizing in your message? You should be doing a little "numbers crunching," shouldn't you?

Considering Point of View

If you think about it, the head of the accounting department is interested in facts and figures, dollars and cents, profit and loss, and the like. These are the pertinent areas of responsibility. (Recall our earlier "right-brain/left-brain" designations.) Therefore, you'll want to slant your message accordingly. When outlining or composing, cost considerations will figure prominently.

Suppose the reader's title were Head of Personnel. Would you do numbers crunching? Where would this reader's self-interests lie?

With *people* concerns. The Head of Personnel is interested in issues such as hiring, firing, staffing, training, EEO, Affirmative Action, employee morale, and so forth. If you were writing to an Engineering Manager, technical concerns would be paramount. Are you starting to get the idea? Good. Now let's complicate things.

What if you're writing one message that will go to a diversity of readers, people exhibiting different sets of self-interests? Now what do you do? I'll give you an example from my personal experience to provide a lesson.

Dense Reports

Right after finishing college in the early 1970's, I began work as a report writer for the New York State Department of Social Services. My bosses figured, "He's the English major, let him do the writing." (I've come to find, by the way, that English majors are the *last* people who should have responsibility for much business writing.) My periodic reports were read by three types of readers: Welfare Commissioners, Data Processing Chiefs, and Caseworkers. Believe me when I tell you that three more diverse groups of people can't be found on planet Earth. These folks had very little in common with one another, except for drawing biweekly paychecks from the same agency, although some of the commissioners had at one time been caseworkers.

For months, I made the tactical mistake of writing prose narrative reports that droned on and on — not knowing any differently and not having been taught any better in school — which failed to take into account my readers' different sets of self-interests. As a result, I was unconsciously mixing information of interest primarily to one group with that intended for the other two groups. I was adept at categorizing the data by subject matter, *but not by readership.* In other words, my three sets of readers had to read *everything* in my reports — even information of no interest to them — because I didn't sort out the data, didn't organize and target it effectively.

The upshot was that people referred to my reports only superficially rather than reading them in-depth. They didn't enjoy having to go through the reports. And they were, in essence, being forced to make mental notes about what information was intended for them, separating it from the rest of the information as they waded through the documents. Not a very pleasant experience. What could I have done — and what did I begin doing — differently?

Organize by Readership

After a few months of overhearing behind–my–back complaints about the way I was writing the reports (where were these people when the page was *blank*?), a revolutionary way to improve them dawned on me. I want to emphasize that it wasn't the substance of the documents that was troublesome or of little interest for my readers. Rather, my *style* of presentation was sorely lacking.

I began categorizing my report contents not only by subject matter but by readership. I was able to break out the reports this way: The first third for Welfare Commissioners, the middle third for Data Processing Chiefs, and the final third for Caseworkers. I cut everybody's reading load by two–thirds. People could now read only the section most pertinent to their self–interests. Certainly, they were free to read any other part of the reports, but the point is that they *no longer had to.* I attached an Executive Summary to everybody's report for overview purposes.

Who's Who

I'm not suggesting that you can immediately begin following my lead and reorganize your reports so that they're segmented by reader group. Policy dictates at your place of employment must be adhered to, and format requirements may not allow for much deviation from the norm. But you can, within document sections, give the data particular reader emphasis simply by keeping in mind who's going to have primary responsibility for reading — and responding to — the information in those sections.

I'll offer another example: a complaint–letter situation. An unhappy car owner is writing to a Detroit automaker about unsatisfactory service he received on chassis undercoating. He's addressing his concern to the head of consumer affairs, really chewing the reader out. About to mail the letter, he asks his wife to look it over. She asks him, "What kinds of letters does a head of consumer affairs typically receive?"

Angry letters, indistinguishable from one another. So her husband tries a different tack. He rewrites the letter, portraying himself as a Woody Allen–type character, stumbling through life at the mercy of automobile service shops. He makes it as funny and as sympathetic as he can, completely changing the tone.

Less than a week later, he gets a phone call from the reader in Detroit, assuring him that his complaint will be resolved. And the reader tells our writer that his was the only letter received recently *not* taking the consumer affairs head to task. In fact, the reader got such a kick out of the letter, he passed it around the office. Here's an example of a typical "win–win" situation. A problem gets solved, and everybody's happy.

Disturbing Trend

I'm a little disturbed by a palpable trend in business these days, one which marks too many superior–subordinate relationships as adversarial. Don't look upon the boss as a foe. Your attitude will only come through between the lines in your message. Even if you don't personally get along, ultimately you're each on the same side. View the reader or listener as a *potential ally* who you're trying to get into your camp. Address the issue from a business point of view. If you're the boss, review messages objectively, and offer only constructive criticism. That way, communication is kept on a professional level, and nobody has to take things personally.

Question #2 – What Will Be Significant for my Audience?

In other words, you're asking, *What does my audience need to know?* We've already begun answering this question. For example, your readers or listeners need to know why they are receiving your message (your objective or purpose), its benefits, and the degree of their involvement; i.e., what you'll want them to do, if anything.

But you'll likely want to take your message beyond these initial concerns. More depth is probably necessary to give your audience a *complete* understanding of significance.

Ask "So What?"

I can best illustrate this point by giving you an example that left the reader wondering, "So what?" During an audit report writing workshop at a bank in Los Angeles, I was reviewing a management summary for one of the participants.   The summary would become part of an analysis in a memo, from which a final report would be derived. In composing his workpapers the auditor had written this statement:

> *"The branch manager had only been in her new position for six weeks."*

As is typically the case for most of us, when transcribing information from draft stage to revision, we seldom rewrite drastically, seldom question what we first wrote. The inclination is to let it stand. But note that the above statement begs the question, "So what?" How is the information significant? What are the implications?

When I asked the auditor these same questions, he thought for a moment, and then told me, "*Since the branch manager had only been in her new position for six weeks, we could not hold her responsible for knowing all the fraud control procedures."* My response was, "The way you just said it is the way to write it."

The auditor's oral statement tells you something, rounding out your understanding completely.   I've gotten to the stage when composing draft revisions (not first drafts, where I just idea dump) that I'll review every paragraph, and most sentences, from the "So what?" perspective.   If what I've written doesn't answer the question, I question its significance in my message. Usually, I then get rid of that paragraph or sentence. If my gut tells me I must keep the idea, then I rework what I've written to make it significant for my audience.

Declarative vs. Imperative

A cue to help you make this process work is to recognize flat, incomplete, declarative statements in your early drafts. *Declarative* statements, as Miss Thistlebottom taught us back in grade school, merely proclaim a point. I refer to them as statements of this ilk: "The sky is blue." They usually don't add much to our store of knowledge, they're not very useful, and they have a static quality. You read one and you wonder — So what?

But with just a little sidespin, by completing a half-formed thought or telling your audience members more of what they need to know, your statements become dynamic, comprehensive (as well as comprehensible), and *telling*.

Be careful to check for declarative sentences or paragraphs when composing recommendations. Prefer *imperative* statements, which impart directives. For example, in a technical report, these two recommendations appeared together:

> "*Use expanded joints in fossil-fueled power plants to minimize water inleakage.*"

> "*For PWR nuclear plants, rolled joints have an added reliability.*"

The first statement reads like a recommendation. It's *imperative*, telling the reader to do something, and including a reason why (a *benefit*). Is the second statement a recommendation? It might have been intended as such, but it loses its significance punch because it's worded declaratively. Keep all your recommendations consistent and parallel by informing the audience of the "So what?" Here's how to revise the second statement:

> "*Use rolled joints in PWR nuclear plants to add reliability.*"

Outline Check

When trying to determine what's significant for your audience before you've composed sentences or paragraphs for reworking, check your outline. Do the points you want to make appear there? If not, should you expand the outline to incorporate more message? The more thorough your outline, the easier it is to develop paragraphs — to pull them from what your outline suggests — later in the *Body*.

Question #3 – How Will the Audience Interpret my Message?

This is the most important question in the profile. And I'm going to answer it right away. Interpretation hinges on the language you use; therefore, keep your language *familiar.* Readers or listeners have very little other than the words they see or hear as tools to dig out the meaning of your message. Make it easy on them. Don't use abstract or complicated language that will miss the mark. Be careful of specialized argot or jargon that might cause misinterpretations.

A Matter of Interpretation

I always tell workshop participants that the easiest thing to achieve in business is a misunderstanding. It's happened to all of us: We say or write something one way, but the message isn't received as intended; it's taken the wrong way.

Certainly, interpretations can be affected by tone of voice, body language, or facial expressions when spoken messages are delivered. In fact, these variables may do more to influence interpretation than the wording of the message. And in written communications, reading between the lines to get at the real or hidden message can often be readily accomplished.

But the wording exerts overriding influence on just what messages ultimately mean to their receivers. Controlling the outcome to the sender's advantage is a function of the ability to demonstrate command of the language. Part of what inhibits desired interpretation is that every profession speaks to itself in its own language, and there is no Rosetta stone — no universal means of translation.

Particular Patois

Now, it's normal, even healthy, for members of groups or professions to devise their own special terminology. Neighborhood residents do it, prisoners do it, lawyers do it. Problems crop up when we slip into what I dub the "Tower of Babble" syndrome: using language reserved for a group with people *outside* the group.

Throughout mankind's history, language has been used to

mark members of so-called "in" groups and to designate outsiders. A certain credibility is even associated with one's ability to "speak the language." It shows, fairly or unfairly, the credentials for group membership. Language has been used to exclude unwanted people from certain groups. In fact, language is a very powerful, very emotional tool used toward varied ends.

Role of Language

I'd like to spend a bit more time on this aspect of the audience profile than on the other four questions because of the critical role language plays in message sending. I'll discuss why familiar language is a linchpin in gaining audience understanding and reaction by using a number of examples I've collected over the years from actual business communications.

Let's start off with a statement from an engineer's report:

> *"The proper functioning of this component
> is critically dependent upon its
> maintaining dimensional integrity."*

No, my fingers didn't hit the wrong keys. That's a for-real, honest-to-God statement. Hard to figure out what the engineer means, isn't it? When I ask people for their interpretation, I usually get blank stares. Then, on urging, someone will gamely take a stab at it.

The statement usually prompts as many different interpretations as there are people reading or hearing it. Is that what the engineer intended? One popular translation is, "This part must be positioned properly." Better, but not quite specific enough. Others range from "Keep the thing together" (?) to "Don't fool around with the shape of whatever." (My favorite!)

Just what is *whatever*? What is a *component*? When I pressed the engineer, he told me he meant:

> *"This part will not work if broken."*

Simple enough, isn't it? Why didn't he write that in the first place? Well, let's see, because it doesn't sound technical enough? Because it's too direct and understandable? Because it doesn't demonstrate a large vocabulary?   Because it doesn't sound impressive enough? But shouldn't we be communicating to *express* and not to *impress*? Questions well worth pondering.

As a classic example of legalese for which I could find no parallel, I must include a municipal law as originally drafted, but revised before enactment. First, the original:

> *"No one shall operate a restaurant unless said proprietor*
> *shall cause to be conspicuously displayed and*
> *maintained at all times a menu, bill of fare, card*
> *or other form or device which shall clearly*
> *indicate to the purchaser the price of the article*
> *or food to be sold or served, which said menu,*
> *bill of fare, card or other like form or device*
> *shall be so placed, displayed and maintained*
> *as to be clearly within the vision of the*
> *purchaser of said article or articles of food at*
> *the time such food is ordered."*

Now the revision, in plain English:

> *"A person cannot run a restaurant unless the*
> *food prices are clearly stated in writing and*
> *the buyer can see them when ordering."*

Subconscious Emotional Appeal

Even though I enjoy picking on the arcane language used by members of the legal profession (aren't attorneys, like politicians and public utilities, fair game?), I'm the first to admit that legal bombast can have a powerful intimidating effect. The IRS know this, and uses it in collection notifications. For example, say you receive in the mail a legal document which opens, *"Know all men by these presents, addressee must show cause in a court of law . . . ."* The phrasing will get your attention. It will also get your adrenalin levels up and your heart beating faster.

Very often, messages that start like this conclude, *". . . failure* to respond will leave us no alternative but to take further appropriate legal action." Notice the open-ended quality of that statement. How do you interpret the meaning? By design on the part of the sender, it can mean whatever dire things your imagination can conjure up. Maybe you don't want to risk finding out what "further appropriate legal action" means. So you comply. Case closed . . . you hope.

Didn't I Hear This on *Hill Street Blues*?

Here's another one, an example of how each profession speaks to itself in its own language. This is an example of "cop talk" written by a desk sergeant in a report: "*The alleged perpetrator emerged from the edifice.*" Meaning? "*The suspect came out of the building.*" Why not just write that in the first place? Because, the sergeant's superiors — precinct commander, chief — write and speak the same way, and he, subconsciously, mimics that style.

In fact, sociologists call such imitative behavior "patterning"; they tell us we imitate or mimic not only language patterns exhibited by those up the chain of command from us, but modes of dress, gestures, hair styles . . . we even tend to drive the same kinds of cars and live in the same kinds of houses (provided they're paying us enough to afford it!).

Interestingly, the human species tends to base much of its behavior not on its own wants or desires so much as on *the ways it thinks others expect it to behave.* For example, what happens when you approach a four-way stop intersection? (If you're driving that Ferrari I mentioned before, you do a lot of downshifting!) The law expects you to stop and look before proceeding. And law-abiding drivers do; it's in their self-interests. Don't you expect other drivers to stop in turn, too?

If you've gotten a reputation as the life of the party, you'll tend to live up to it because of this subconscious expectation-fulfillment phenomenon. And, as many of you well know, it can be darned exhausting.

Sender and Receiver Working Together

I try to demonstrate in my messages a correlation for my audience, a dovetailing of their self-interests and mine, their expectations and mine. The best way is to keep the language familiar and convey the understanding that we're all on the same side. Listeners at a talk in which the next example appeared didn't arrive at that understanding. They were all loan officers at an S&L who heard a senior vice-president make the statement:

> *"If we find the reasonable probability of repayment*
> *out of reach, we will have to respond in terms of*
> *extension of future credit."*

Half the listeners thought it meant, "If they can't pay what they owe, we'll have to lend them more money." The other half thought it meant, "If they can't pay what they owe, we will *not* lend them more money." Completely opposite interpretations are possible. Who's right? Suppose half the listeners act one way based on their interpretation and half another way? They'll be acting at cross-purposes, and that can have serious ramifications. The problem lies with the phrase, "to respond in terms of extension of future credit." The language isn't abstract, it's just vague. In other words, it's open to interpretation. When you're trying to get audience members to act as a team, everyone's interpretation must be the same.

Shifting Your Brain Into "Park"

See if you can make heads or tails of what's contained in this sentence from a memo:

> *"Please reconsider Mr. Harder's salary remuneration*
> *wherein inordinate incentives to ignore*
> *nonproductive responsibilities are not apparent."*

Nothing induces brain fade as surely as a gem like that one. You have to shift mental gears too many times to keep up. So you give up. What does it mean? Your guess is as good as mine. I'm sure the writer thought he was conveying a meaningful idea, but on second reading you'll probably exclaim, "Oh, come on!" Depending on who the message sender is in relation to you, you may even begin to feel a bit intimidated. Here's what you begin thinking: "Let's see, the writer is a company big-wig with an MBA from Harvard making $300,000 a year. Gee, if I don't understand the message, there must be something wrong with me." Well, there's nothing wrong with you — necessarily, that is. Quite simply, the statement is overly complex: too many *20-dollar* words when plain old *2-dollar* words will suffice.

Conceptual Smokescreens

When I encounter brain-twisters as a reader or listener, I'm reminded of something the early-20th Century economist and social observer Thorstein Veblen said: "The more complex the language used to describe an endeavor, the more likely the endeavor to be make-believe." It's good practice to get your antennae out when you bump up against high complexity. I've become wary over the years, wondering, "Why am I being bamboozled?"

Usually, impenetrable messages are attempts to create a smoke-screen, obscuring the reality that either: A) the sender has absolutely no idea what he or she is trying to say; or B) the sender is trying to hide something.

Alice in Wonderland commented to the March hare, when questioned about the meaning of a word, that a word means just what she wants it to, nothing more and nothing less. Well, that way lies madness, unless someone is living an Alice-in-Wonderland existence. (Unfortunately, in many cases, that's not too far-fetched an assessment.)

Use Familiar Language

The rest of us, though, need to precisely and accurately communicate in language that triggers immediate recognition: *familiar* language. Again, the greater your working vocabulary, the more flexibility of expression you can demonstrate. I don't always use plain language exclusively. Sometimes I deem the occasion appropriate for dressing the language up in finery. But I guard against overblown vocabulary. It's okay to send your words out in a tux now and then, but don't deck them out in foolish clowns' outfits.

Am I suggesting you never use specific or technical terminology for fear that some readers could miss your meaning? No. Fields such as Medicine and Geophysics, for instance, have necessarily developed highly particular vocabularies, and for good reason. Sometimes the only way to convey exact meaning is to precisely distinguish wording. Mark Twain warned that the difference between *lightning* and *lightning bug* is vast. So let's choose the right word, even though there may be subtle shades of differences.

Take the meanings of *idiosyncracy* and *eccentricity*. A dictionary points out that both involve divergence from the normal or customary in thought or action. But *eccentricity* emphasizes strangeness while *idiosyncracy* strongly suggests individuality and independence of action. An excellent rule of thumb when making language choices is to consult a dictionary. When in doubt, check it out.

I don't mean to belabor this third question in the audience profile. But my lingering emphasis grows out of the critical nature of the effect language has on interpretation. No more crucial determinant of style permeates the effectiveness of communications than *familiar language*.

Learning by Doing

Here's an opportunity to participate in interaction with me (as I suggested in the Preface). Try to unravel the knotty meanings of the statements below, statements rendered nearly unrecognizable because of how complex, how abstract, the language is. (When you're ready to give up, you'll find an answer sheet following.)

a. Undue velocity produces lavish prodigality.

b. An overabundance of culinary experts
   often vitiates the boullion.

c. A mineral matter of various composition,
   when engaged in periodic revolutions,
   exhibits no tendency to accumulate any
   of the cryptogamic plants of the class Musci.

    d. It is not considered prudent to enumerate an
      individual's stock of domestic fowl in advance
      of the termination of the period of gestation.

    e. A pair offers the possibility of companionship,
      while triple identities considered as an aggregate
      assume the overpowering characteristics of
      a multitude.

The translations:

    a. Haste makes waste.

    b. Too many cooks spoil the broth.

    c. A rolling stone gathers no moss.

    d. Don't count your chickens before they're
      hatched.

    e. Two's company, three's a crowd.

Question #4 – What Are my Audience Members' Personal Characteristics?

This, in some ways, is a spinoff of the first question in the profile. Sometimes a person's title or position can fill in the blanks on who that audience member is as a person. For example, an engineer tends to be technically oriented. If I were composing specifications, I'd want to get the technical details right. Remember that certain professions demand certain types of people, just as certain types of people gravitate toward certain professions.

But I also want to know more outside the professional context, taking into account the personal. For instance, try to determine whether your audience:

- takes the short- or long-term view
- tends to be budget-conscious
- exhibits a sense of humor
- likes messages chock full of detail

■ is highly analytical
■ takes tough stands
■ is easy to get along with

Asking additional questions might be highly appropriate.

No Stone Unturned

What if the questions aren't easy to answer or are unanswerable? Don't be too quick to give up. You've still got a few more stones to unturn. Even if you don't know your audience members personally, if you think about it, you do know some things generally about people in the working world. Have you ever met anyone who isn't busy, who doesn't appreciate clear, concise, understandable messages? Of course, the more specific your focus, the better the chances for success.

For example, I once wrote a letter to a phone company sales manager in Denver who had played professional football a few years earlier. I married both sets of data in my message: sales manager and former athlete. My strategy, even though I didn't know the reader personally, was to use language that would set off immediate associations for him. I wrote about developing a team game plan, eliminating interference, keeping our ultimate goal in mind. I tried not to be corny, and I tried not to overdo it. My sports metaphor accomplished positive results: I received a favorable response from the reader.

Now, I'm not saying I wouldn't have had I not known he played pro ball at one time. But that knowledge was icing on the cake. Because I took a little bit extra time to prepare, to dig and find out more about my reader, I got the desired results.

You Know More Than You Think You Do

Suppose you were writing a letter to the president of Xerox Corporation. Do you know the president personally? No? Well, what do you know *about* this person? Nothing? Are you sure? For instance, are you writing to a man or a woman? Black or white? Over age 50 or under? High-school dropout or college graduate? Low-handicap golfer or duffer?

How can you answer these questions, you wonder, and what difference do they make anyway? Well, it's probably a safe assumption that the president of Xerox is *not* a Spanish-surnamed, black female with an eighth-grade education. Now, she may be about to make the cut on the LPGA tour, but how likely is it? You probably *do* know much more than you may think about your audience's personal characteristics, especially if you have only an inkling of how the corporate world works. And we know that, for good or ill, the upper echelons of the business world are inhabited largely by white, late middle-aged males.

CEO composites, compiled by organizations like Standard & Poors, give demographic details in depth of executive-suite top dogs. In addition to what we already know and can surmise about them, these men tend to be Northeast or Midwest natives, Protestant, married to the same woman for more than twenty years, and they've likely attended either Ivy League or large state university colleges. A high proportion of them got their career start in sales. (But, these days, this picture is changing.)

Filling In the Blanks

Certainly, it can be dangerous to stereotype, especially when stereotyping doesn't helpfully fill in the blanks for us, as it sometimes can. If, for instance, you're preparing a talk for pediatric-care nurses, you can safely assume that a good number of the audience will be female, will have a health-care background, will find fulfillment from interacting with children, and so on. Some of these assumptions are even patently obvious. But it's usually what's right under our noses that we most tend to ignore. The difficulty arises when personal characteristics are *not* so apparent. What do you do then?

My advice is, don't worry about it. This fourth question in the profile isn't as important as, for example, the third. So you need not spend inordinate amounts of time trying to answer it. Certainly, it's not worth holding up message composition if you don't have answers in detail.

Remember that, since you're trying to sell in an <u>Action</u> message, you need only gain a general grasp of the audience, as market researchers do when assessing buyer demographics. For your <u>Info only</u> communications, substance outweighs audience personal characteristics.

Question #5 – How Can I Get the Reaction I Seek?

This is the final question in the profile and, perhaps, the most difficult to answer. If we knew unfailingly how to get audience reactions, a very disturbing result would occur: This book would be rendered unnecessary. But I take heart because getting reactions is typically a hit–or–miss, frustrating proposition. Yet you, too, can take heart because I'm going to point out ways of succeeding. First, let's address the critical concerns.

Pulling It All Together

If you'll look back at step #5 under getting organized (Chapter 1, page 24), you'll recall that the sought–after reaction is already defined.   For example, we want our boss to approve purchasing the IBM Personal System 2 for the department. Now, how do we get the boss to do just that?   Well, we've already begun answering the question. We're going to follow each of the five steps detailed in **Organizing the Message** (discussed in Chapter 1) to achieve this end. Of special import are coming up with benefits and making the message interesting. And we're going to keep in mind our   reader's   self–interests,   point   out   what's   of   greatest significance, and use familiar language.

So we've already begun answering this final question as part of the pre–composition process.   What we've accomplished is an integrative effort whereby the steps we're going through and the questions we're answering are complementary.

Focusing Your Efforts

All the information I've discussed so far in this book is channeled toward answering the fifth question above in the audience profile. How does our personal experience in other situations enter into our concerns?   Think of times past when you've written successful messages, delivered successful talks, when you've gotten desired reactions from your spouse or dealt effectively with an

obstreperous four-year old. How did you do it? You haven't a clue?
Think now, you've obviously *appealed effectively* each time. Okay,
how can you do it again, systematically, regularly?

Frederick Hertzberg, one of the country's motivation gurus
who's taught at Case Western Reserve University, has developed
what he calls a "KITR Theory": You can get people to do your bidding
through a Kick In The Rear. And it works. KITR is highly effective
when you have authority, when you're dealing with a subordinate,
or when you're bigger than the other guy. KITR, like totalitarianism,
does work, but we have to ask, *at what cost?* In the short term, you
can most definitely get others to do what you want by using force,
threats, discipline. Sometimes (rarely, I hope), they're the only way,
a last resort. But they're not the only *strategic* way, and can very
often, as we know, function as dealkillers.

Nothing squelches employee morale or camaraderie faster than
a martinet supervisor who uses a variation of KITR to manage by
intimidation rather than by inspiration . . . even if this supervisor is
a benevolent autocrat! (You know the type: Someone people love to
use, but hate to report to.)

KITR, though, doesn't work very well in the long term. It can
squelch morale. A more effective method for getting the reaction you
want — in addition to each of the processes discussed so far — is to
structure the message carefully. The next chapter deals with
structural elements you can master in fairly simple fashion to help
put your best foot forward in composing and delivering result-
oriented messages.

Chapter 2 Review

The significant points presented in this chapter are:

   ☞   Profile your audience; keep in mind their
        self interests by asking:
        – Who is my audience?
        – What will be significant?
        – How will the message be
          interpreted?
        – What are audience members'

personal characteristics?
– How can I get my reaction?

☞   Keep in mind that people do things for their reasons,
      not yours. You *can* be persuasive, but only when you
      learn to communicate primarily from the perspective
      of your audience.

"There's a better way: Find it."
                - Anonymous

Overview

In this chapter, I'll talk about the third system or process to follow in developing a procedure for preparing your oral or written message: How to *structure* your composition in a better way than you may now be doing. It'll be time to start on more of the interactive exercises I want to involve you in, too. So get pen, paper, and thinking cap ready.

```
┌─────────────────────────────────────┐
│                                     │
│        The Third Process:           │
│        Think STRUCTURE              │
│                                     │
└─────────────────────────────────────┘
```

Use four essential building blocks common to any writing or speaking preparation task in composing an ordered communication, one which prompts the desired audience reaction. I'll go into considerable detail on each of the following elements:

Tone - This means attitude. Control it by using ingredients detailed under **Message Mechanics** (beginning on page 51) to affect the outcome of your message.

Opening - The introductory portion of your message. Here's where you state your purpose and briefly overview the remainder of the message. Then, provide a context or focal point for the audience to get its bearings and be able to follow along. Your opening will provide a pathway through the rest of the document.

Body - This is the heart of your message, where you include detailed documentation and substantiation. You'll best compose it by following guidelines discussed under **Content Mapping** (see Chapter 4).

Closing - Your final point of impact with the audience. Use the closing to reinforce or summarize key points, as necessary. For example, when you're ready to conclude discussion, I'll point out three convenient categories into which you can slot your closing thoughts.

Each part of an oral or written message can be self-contained; that is, it can include its own *Opening, Body,* and *Closing* with a consistent *Tone* threaded throughout. This application helps you break up any kind of lengthy presentation into bite-size chunks or consolidated units. The intent is to make the task of sending — and that of receiving — the message a piecemeal, easy-to-accomplish process.

Let's look more closely, then, at each of the structural elements and begin determining which informed choices are necessary to help achieve your goals. And remember that practice is going to help bind these individual elements together as worthwhile, truly usable tools. So be ready to jump in when I cue you as we now begin moving from process concerns to product concerns. We've drawn up blueprints, materials are at hand, and excavation has begun. Now you're at the juncture of starting to put a message in place where none has existed before.

> ## Structural Element Number
> ## One: Tone – Attitude

Much of what each of us learned about the English language and about communicating, from grade school on, can be termed **Message Mechanics.** Four mechanical ingredients are of special concern because they not only establish your *Tone,* or attitude (in other words, the way you come across), they also help to make your message interesting. You'll recall that when I was discussing step #4 in the organizing process associated with pre-composition (Chapter 1, page 21), I mentioned keeping this concern of how to add interest on a side burner. Well, let's move it to a front position. How do you project a desired tone and at the same time make your message interesting to read or listen to?

Attuned To Tone

Whether we're aware of it or not, our communications do convey a certain tone. In fact, the old adage that audiences don't react so much to what our message says as to how the message is conveyed — and received — is simply a variation on what I've been emphasizing all along in this book: Style counts as much as if not more than substance.   You can control the tone by knowing what it's made up of and making choices to best suit your objectives.   Plus, you can draw your audience in with these same ingredients.   The four **Message Mechanics** are:

1) **Vocabulary (Language)** – These two words are synonyms. Your vocabulary is the set of words you use to communicate.   Some educational researchers and semantics scholars estimate that a working vocabulary of about 500 words is necessary to get by as a functionally literate adult in American society.   (I wonder, "*Which* 500?") That's not very many. Consider, by contrast, that a typical college graduate has a working vocabulary in the neighborhood of 25,000 words.

The most professional wordsmiths among us, those with supposedly the best-developed vocabularies, probably have an understanding of 45,000-60,000 words at their command. Who are some of these people? William F. Buckley clones? Most are writers, journalists, editors, English professors — people you'd expect to have to demonstrate in-depth knowledge of words and their meanings.

But even these latter figures pale when you consider that the English language contains over 800,000 words. Granted, many are extremely scientific or technical, and many more are so abstruse as not to be needed in everyday usage.   But look at it this way: Even the best-educated and most knowledgeable among us know only 5 percent or so of all the words there are to know.   Of course, even if you could call up the meanings of hundreds of thousands of words, that wouldn't necessarily make you an effective communicator.

Harmony Of Parts

The trick is knowing which words are appropriate, and when to use them. This issue is akin to asking whether all 88 keys on a piano keyboard are really necessary. And why are there 88?   Why not 73 or 104? (Yes, there are 11 octaves of 8 notes each. But why *those* numbers?) Numbers don't really matter, beyond a minimum, that is. Piano-playing ability is not based on being able to identify the musical notes each key plays.   Melody and harmony come from mastering the right combination.

So what's the right combination of words to use in message sending? Before we go any further, let's define the term "word." What's a word? (To a software programmer the answer is 16 bits.) Is a word simply a device we use to *hide* what we really mean?

Again, what's a word?

Have you come to a halt? It's funny, isn't it: We use words many times each day in speech and writing, and yet we're hard pressed to offer a definition. You might be saying to yourself, "Well, let's see, a word is a thought, isn't it? An idea?" That's partly right. Okay, you think, a word is a group of letters that convey a meaning. Again, partly right. If, finally, you consult a dictionary, you find there that a word is a symbol for an idea. In other words, a word is like a map to a territory.

What we tend to overlook, though, is that the map is not the territory; the symbol is not the idea itself. I've already said that words have tremendous power. It isn't true that "sticks and stones may break my bones but words will never hurt me." Words *can* hurt. Think of profanities, racial epithets, contexts that can do real damage . . . if we let them. If someone says to me, "Your idea stinks," my feelings may be hurt, and I may be on the defensive. But that doesn't mean my idea stinks. I have to maintain perspective. We sometimes assign validity to words invalidly.

To illustrate: Some unkind, untactful person may call me stupid, but that doesn't make me stupid. Eleanor Roosevelt once said that no one can make us feel inferior without our permission. Okay, scant consolation, maybe, but you see the point I'm trying to make.

On The Other Hand . . .

What if someone calls me smart? Much as I hate to admit it, that statement doesn't make me smart. So don't merely take words at face value. Think before you assign validity, and take into account the broader context. We all learned a valuable lesson in youth from the *boy who cried wolf* fable. Just because he said he saw a wolf doesn't mean he did. Suppose someone you knew as a practical joker burst into your office at work yelling "Fire!" You might tend to look for further evidence before assigning validity, or belief, to the message. You'd want to smell smoke or see flames. (Of course, you could get burned if the guy, this one time, isn't joking!)

But suppose a city fireman in helmet and rubber jacket, holding fire hose in hand, burst into your office yelling "Fire!" You probably wouldn't look for further evidence before taking to the exit. Yet there still may not be a fire. The map is not the territory.

When I was discussing the audience profile, question #3 (Chapter 2, page 36), I emphasized using familiar language. Descriptive vocabulary, especially, can provide this broader, more understandable context to which I'm referring. You may even find that, in devising a language map for your audience, you have an ability to paint pictures with words, to simplify and de-mystify.

Context As Canvas

I recently conducted a training seminar with a group of technicians who manufacture pacemakers. Among the initial steps physicians take when implanting these devices in patients is to push the start button. This step showed up in the user manual as, "Depress the start button." What does that mean — give it a bad day, make it feel sad?

Speaking of physicians, think of what's really being communicated in a post-operative report written by a surgeon who lost a patient when this explanation is given:

"The patient failed to resuscitate."

I get a sense the doctor is trying to sidestep blame.

I take a lesson from Albert Einstein who, when explaining the concept of nuclear fission (the opposite of fusion), stayed away from complex scientific terminology, particularly with non-technical audiences. Einstein likened the process of nuclear fission to shooting pool. In billiards, when a cue ball strikes a rack of balls, it breaks the rack apart, sending the balls caroming around the pool table. A similar process occurs when a force strikes an atom and breaks it up into smaller molecules.

Understanding Simplified

Note the mental association that's easy to make with Einstein's explanation. I'm not saying it's good nuclear physics, but it is effective communication, and a basic understanding is all the uninitiated need, anyway.

I remember first being introduced to computer operations in the early 1970's while working at the Social Services Department. The chief of data processing didn't resort to arcane jargon when explaining to me how a computer works. Instead, he asked me to think of the computer as a brain. His strategy worked. We all have at least a basic familiarity with how the brain functions. So it's not difficult to make the mental leap to understand that a computer functions much like a brain: it can store data in memory, recognize and retrieve information, calculate, and so on. Suddenly, computers become much less intimidating and inhibiting because of the way in which they're explained.

Try these tactics when you're putting together first drafts of your messages. Ask yourself, How would I say this "in other words"? Keep it clear and simple. You need not worry about originality or creativity; rather, you're striving for concreteness instead of abstraction. Often, it's precisely abstraction that impedes understanding. For example, I remember seeing a bank credit report which listed, as collateral on a loan, a "ranch asset" worth $100,000. What's a ranch asset? A full silo, a thrasher, a farmer's wife? It turned out that the loan officer was obliquely alluding to a prize bull. My advice was to so specify, to take the language by the horns and call a bull a bull.

Is there certain vocabulary to avoid in message sending? Well, this question raises the red flag of personal preference. For instance, I've noticed over the past fifteen years or so that corporate America has developed a fascination with three-word groupings like "cost-benefit analysis," "optimal digital synchronization," "price-earnings ratio," and so forth. The first two words are usually hyphenated adjectives. (One of my favorites in this genre is "high reliability condenser design study" — four unhyphenated adjectives.) The groupings sound impressive, admittedly, but I'm not sure they say much. If the users find an immediate meaning inherent, fine, I'll back off.   But, again, my criterion for usage is to ask, "Would I say this in ordinary conversation? *Really?*"

Eliminating Friction From Idea Flow

I will suggest a type of vocabulary overuse to avoid: excessive nouns. You may recall Miss Thistlebottom saying in grade school that a noun is the name of a person, place, or thing. Nouns merely label; they have static quality. Unfortunately, they've been creeping into written and oral communications for a long, long time. It's way past time to do some excising. Why? Because by changing nouns to verbs (action words), you do much to propel your audience through your message, making it more concise and easier to follow as you do so. Verbs have a dynamic quality. I liken them to lubricants which smooth the flow of thoughts. Nouns, on the other hand, create friction, slowing the audience down.

Stay alert for words you use that have these suffixes:

ion   ment   ance

These little letter groupings coming at the end of words (prefixes come at the beginning) signal nouns. By changing them to verbs you can revise a statement like "*It is our recommendation that*" to become "*We recommend.*" Try your hand at changing the nouns in the following phrases to verbs:

He has qualifications for
She suggested issuance of a certificate
We made a replacement
Can you make a determination
To be in compliance with
The director had an announcement

2) Verb Voice – A verb is not only the action word in a sentence, it's also the most important word.   You can't strictly have a sentence in English without a verb, and a verb by itself can be a sentence. If I say to you "Go!" you know what I mean.   I'm not saying you can't convey a complete thought without a verb.   Say your response to my directive is "Where?" You've asked a one-word question without using a verb, and I know what you mean. I may even point and say "There." We're having a conversation, even though we're not communicating in complete sentences. In fact, we don't always have to use verbs or even words to send messages. All of us have heard of non-verbal communicating. A moan, a nod of the head, a facial expression— each can convey a meaningful message, and each existed long before formal spoken or written language came into being.

But I digress.

Back To Basics

Well, maybe I'm not digressing too much. Because I am discussing elements of message sending in general and of sentences in particular. Nouns and verbs, when used in sentences, take on the roles of subject (or object) and predicate. What's important is establishing and then understanding the relationship between subject and predicate in sentences. Here's where *verb voice* comes in. This, incidentally, won't be news to you. In fact, all the **Message Mechanics** ingredients represent familiar ground. If you plug in the memory circuits you'll recall having been taught this in school. The problem is, the information wasn't packaged in such a way as to make it stand out, to distinguish it as useable. We tended to be taught concepts, and to have to learn them, in a vacuum. Let's open up our mental capacities.

Verbs are written and spoken in either the active or passive voice. Active means the subject in the sentence is doing the action in the verb. Passive means the subject is receiving the action. I liken active to pitching and passive to catching. Look at these examples:

Active	Passive
I wrote the letter.	The letter was written by me.
We saved money.	Money was saved by us.

Active	Passive
The managers will change procedures.	Procedures will be changed by the managers.
Consider these points.	Consideration should be given to these points.

Note that each sentence, whether in active or passive voice, says the same thing. But the active version is concise and direct. It puts the doer (the subject) up front, which is how we tend to speak. The passive version flip–flops the active, adding words and changing the emphasis. Very rarely do we tend to speak in the passive voice. It's not as economical and it's indirect. I must point out that I'm not assigning value to either rendering; please don't infer that I'm suggesting Active is good and Passive is bad. I'm simply stating that the active voice gets you, and your audience, to the point quickly.

Sometimes, the active voice may be considered blunt or too direct. If you deem it inappropriate, then by all means go ahead and use the passive. Effective communicators know the difference between the two voices, and how and when to use either. They're able to exercise flexibility and sensitivity to demands of tact or political considerations. To illustrate: my audience profile may tell me that the people to whom I'm sending my message are subordinates who want me to shoot from the hip in no uncertain terms. I'll use active voice in that case. But on another occasion I may assess the audience as superiors, all of whom would appreciate notes of deference in my message. Here's where I'd choose passive voice.

Exercise Time

The next exercise shows five sentences written in passive voice. Rewrite each to make it active:

> a. The combination for opening the safe was forgotten by me.

b. Rates were found to be varied by
the standards committee.

c. When shutoff occurs the equipment is
programmed to perform an orderly restart.

d. These amounts are considered
to be insignificant when compared to
the ultimate total.

e. Our first association meeting will always
be remembered by everyone in attendance.

Now, let's see how you did. I'll show you suggested revisions for each sentence, with explanatory comments where necessary. Keep in mind that I'm not presenting a set of "correct" answers. There's no right or wrong when it comes to verb voice, rather *effective* or *ineffective*.

Revisions

a. I forgot the safe combination.

(The doer, "I," is up front, where we tend to put ourselves when we speak. Doesn't the original sentence idea order seem convoluted? We can also economize by dropping the phrase "for opening." Opening — or closing — is implied.)

b. The standards committee found various rates. Or,
The standards committee varied the rates.

(Two interpretations are possible. It's hard to know from the original sentence which one is meant. When checking for whether you have a *two-way* meaning, look for the passive voice. Typically, changing to active voice gives the sentence *one-way* direction.)

c. The equipment restarts at shutoff.

(The original implies that someone waits for the equipment to shut off, then programs it to restart. It's probably a safe bet that the equipment is pre-programmed. Question whether the phrase "to perform an orderly" is necessary. Note also that my revision changes "restart" from noun to verb.)

d. We think these amounts are insignificant compared to the totals.

(The original doesn't say that the amounts are insignificant, only that someone thinks they are. But who? The sentence needs a doer to make it active. Another subject might be, "The IRS thinks these amounts are insignificant." Which, of course, is complete folly because the IRS never thinks any amount is insignificant! Note, also, the second passive-voice verb in the original: "when compared." When compared by whom? It's unknown. The revision above keeps "compared" passive, but the implication is that "We" are comparing as well as thinking.

Could we rightfully rewrite the sentence as, "The totals are significant, not these amounts"?)

e. Everyone will always remember our first association meeting.

(Here, I've inverted the ideas and eliminated the *ance* noun.)

A final comment on verb voice: Don't confuse it with verb tense. I often hear people defending their use of the passive by explaining that they're writing or speaking about something that occurred in the past, therefore the passive voice. Voice, though, has nothing to do with tense. You can have future tense and passive voice (for example, "Plans should be made soon").

The next ingredient links up with and expands on voice.

3) Short, Loose Sentences – Let's first define terms before going further with discussion. What is a sentence? An odd collection of words preceding a period? Unfortunately, I see and hear far too many sentences which are little else. If we consult an English handbook, we'll find a clear, possibly even familiar definition: *A* *sentence is a complete thought.* Remember, we can communicate in less than completely formed thoughts, but technically we wouldn't be using sentences to do so. In formal written and spoken communications — a categorization that would apply to most of our business messages — we want to convey meaning and understandability. One of the most effective ways to do this is to prefer sentences which are short and loose.

Granted, "short" is a relative term. Would you consider a man short who stands 6 feet? He'd be in a small percentage of the population in terms of height. Yet if you put him on a basketball court with the starting five of any NBA team, chances are good he'd be one of the shortest people there by many inches, a veritable midget. So, again, we must look to the context to get definition and meaning. When it comes to sentences, short is not only a relative but a slippery term. Length can be all over the place. For example, the French writer Marcel Proust could construct complete thoughts that were more than 900 words long! The playwright Bernard Shaw frequently penned sentences in excess of 150–200 words.

Most of us don't attempt to emulate such prolixity, at least not intentionally. But we often come close to longwindedness. To give you some examples: It's been estimated (I suppose by the sort of people who research such statistics) that the average length of a sentence in a Supreme Court ruling is 38 words. If that doesn't sound terribly long to you, try reading a Supreme Court ruling sometime. If the length of the sentences doesn't present a hurdle, the legalese will. A similar phenomenon awaits if you look over the text contained in your life–insurance policy: long sentences, typically averaging more than 24 words. So what's an ideal length, then? No more than 20 words, on average.

You're wondering, where does the 20 come from? Is that just an arbitrary number? No. In fact, I'm getting 20 from two sources:

> * *Speech therapists*, who tell us that when we talk, our sentences usually average somewhere between 12–16 words.

> * *Behavioral psychologists*, who've found that when people have to read or listen to clusters of

sentences that ramble on for more than 20 words, they lose interest and therefore meaning.

On and On and On . . .

We've all encountered inordinately lengthy sentences in written messages that have forced us to double back over what we just read to make sense out of it. And we've probably been distracted or annoyed at having to do so. Suddenly, we're no longer "with" the writer.

And certainly we've all been subjected to bombasts of verbiage when listening to politicians, official "spokesmen," and Oscar winners. Extremely off-putting, right? The most effective way to manage the message and the audience reaction is to control the flow, to establish a comfortable rhythm for ourselves and those reading or listening to our communications. Try not to go beyond 20 words in a sentence. But don't get caught up in counting every single word as you prepare. Such wasteful effort would defeat the very streamlining purposes you're trying to accomplish.

I have a suggested technique to pass along which I've found very helpful. It gets you to focus not on word count but on the physical space your sentences take up. For example, note this sentence:

> *Remember to get the last of the handouts typed and copied for distribution at the Tuesday evening session in Dallas.*

That sentence contains exactly 20 words. It's two and a half lines long, based on the margins I used. Here's how it looks written in longhand:

Remember to get the last of the handouts typed and copied for distribution at the Tuesday evening session in Dallas.

Now it still takes up two and a half lines. When I'm writing out messages, a buzzer goes off in my head about every two and a half lines to alert me that I'm getting near 20 words. It's time to wrap up my thought and put a period at the end. Of course, I don't always go two and half lines for each sentence. Variety is not only the spice of life, it's a lifesaver to keep you from going over the edge in message sending.

So my next sentence is likely to be only a line or so (about 8 words), and the one following that might be two lines (about 15 words). I don't want monotony to set in, either for me or my audience. I'm aware of changing the sentence pace to maintain interest. Occasionally, it's okay to go beyond 20 words. But don't make it a habit. Condition yourself to be succinct.

You can tailor this advice for yourself by checking the margins you use and the size of your handwriting. For instance, on an 8.5" X 11" sheet of paper, I tend to write 8–10 words a line. If your handwriting is large and expansive, your word count might be half that. If your handwriting is small, you may have 20 words in one line. So experiment a bit. Your handwriting size and the physical space your sentences take up tend to be constants, exhibiting patterns you formed early in life. Remember that a central theme of this book is to monitor behavior patterns and then make choices to modify that behavior accordingly.

Making Word Count Count

What if you compose much of the time or exclusively on a word processor? Simple. You just apply the measuring technique to the physical electronic space your words take up. As I'm preparing this text on a word processor, my 20-word limit is reached in about two lines, approximating — for me — the amount of space my handwritten sentences take up.

One adjunct to all this information about short sentences: spoken sentences, as speech therapists tell us, tend to be shorter than written ones, so you may find that you automatically curb garrulousness at the podium. Just make sure that the draft of the speech you're writing or word processing doesn't contain sentences sure to induce brain fade.

Your Type of Sentence

At the same time you're watching sentence length, keep in mind sentence type. Here's where the designation *Loose* comes in. In the Preface, I mentioned that our grade–school teachers taught us four types of sentences: simple, compound, complex, and compound–complex. On top of that, we learned that sentences can be declarative, imperative, interrogative, or exclamatory (which has more to do with purpose than with type). My point is, that's a lot to keep in mind; in fact, it's a lot more than you typically need to know — unless you're an English teacher.

Concentrate instead on whether your sentences are *Loose* or *Periodic*. Simply put, a loose sentence states the main idea up front; in a periodic sentence the main idea comes at the end, just before the period. We'll normally speak in loose sentences, getting to the point economically and running less risk of laryngitis in the process. Unfortunately, too many of our written sentences are periodic, forcing the audience to juggle secondary points before we deliver the payoff. Nobody likes to be kept in suspense (unless reading a mystery story or listening to a joke). Here are examples of both sentence types:

Loose	Periodic
Our stock dropped drastically last week chiefly because of investment losses.	Chiefly because of investment losses, *our stock dropped drastically last week.*
Begin the conversion before consulting the plot chart.	Before consulting the plot chart, *begin the conversion.*
We can process your application once you submit the following information:	We must have certain information to process applications, and because the following information was missing from yours, *we were unable to process it.*

The main idea is italicized in each version. Periodic sentences invert the loose idea order, much the same way that passive voice flip–flops active. When it's preferable to pull no punches, prefer the loose sentence.   On the other hand, for those times when you'd rather lead up to an idea before lowering the boom, use the periodic mode.

Analyzing the dynamics of the third set of sample sentences (page 63) can help make a key point.   The periodic version is from a credit card application follow–up letter. First, it's long (23 words). Second, it forces the reader to suspend secondary information before getting to what's significant. Third, the writer tells the reader what *cannot* be done.   The loose version, by contrast, is concise (11 words), gets right to what's important, and tells the reader what *can* be done by drawing the reader into the action process.   The *Tone* is thereby affected.

Knowing When to Vary the Approach

Of course, much of the world's literature contains sentences written in the periodic mode (e.g., "For want of a horse, a battle was lost").   So there's nothing wrong with a periodic sentence as such. There will be times, in fact, when you may want to provide a buffer between yourself and the message. The periodic sentence allows this. Or you may sense that you'll encounter resistance to your ideas, but you don't want to pussyfoot about stating them.   Here again, the periodic sentence can bail you out.

I tend to take the loose approach when I'm communicating good news, positive information, or data that I'm confident will be favorably received. For bad news, or for those messages that call for tact or political savvy, the periodic approach works well.

All this is not to say that you'll adeptly steer a safe course in message sending by simply appreciating the differences between loose and periodic sentences. Again, you're trying to stack the deck in your favor. There will be times, no matter how judicious your choice of sentence type, when you'll encounter resistance or outright disagreement.   It's naive to assume either result can never occur. But I liken the process of developing these communication skills to muscle building. You use isometrics (weights, Nautilus machines) to work and shape your muscles.   Resistance builds muscle.   So it *can* be desirable.

Accommodating vs. Offending

Besides, what a boring world it would be if everyone always agreed with everyone else. As Mark Twain said, it's difference of opinion that makes horse races. At the very least, when speaking or writing with audiences, we're trying to win over as many (and offend as few) people as possible.   Assess how this opening in a letter written by a bank customer-service clerk achieves this aim:

> *You made a mistake filling out a recent deposit slip.*

The verb, "made," is active voice, and the sentence is short and loose. But what about the tone? Isn't it accusatory? It reads as though the objective is to castigate the customer. A better customer-relations tack would be to deliberately use a longer, passive voice, periodic sentence with different vocabulary. How about this revision:

> *A review of customers' recent deposit slips turned up
> a discrepancy in one of yours.*

Now, the red-flag word "mistake" is softened as "discrepancy," the reader is grouped together with other customers instead of singled out, and the accusatory finger of blame pointed in the original is blunted with the periodic construction. The writer is deflecting away from the reader and onto a review of deposit slips. The blow is softened. Clearly, the objective in the rewrite is to solve a problem.

Time again to exercise your ability to distinguish elements of **Message Mechanics** and apply them. The six sentences below contain not only passive voice, but they're periodic, they're long, and some are wordy. In addition, there's an imbalance of parts inherent in two or three, an imbalance regarding Parallel Structure, which has to do with keeping points uniform and consistent. For example, when discussing multiple items which are similar in nature, keep points parallel by presenting all items using the same part of speech, such as all nouns, all verbs, all participles, and so on. (See the list of action steps, all verbs, in example *d* on page 67.)

For now, rewrite each of the sentences, improving and streamlining the idea flow. Let your imaginations go here. After all, this exercise isn't for keeps. You may decide to break long sentences into 2 or 3 shorter ones, or use lists. (After the exercise I'll present suggested revisions and discuss each with you so you can make comparisons and measure your own progress.)

a. To facilitate the identification of samples,
   all samples should be numbered as follows:

b. A $4000 monthly charge is assessed
   by the service company for computer
   time and printed output and to
   maintain the system.

c. Pursuant to our conversation, I shall endeavor
   to realize, at the earliest possible date, an
   equitable return on your investment utilizing
   all of the resources available to the firm.

d. Steps must be taken to remove phosphates from
   waste materials, devising a means for early
   detection of oil spills, and enactment of laws to
   prohibit dumping of industrial waste.

e. Since the implementation of the program, it
   has become increasingly apparent that
   participation in the program is not at this
   time economically feasible due to the low
   percentage of approval that has been realized
   on these applications.

f. Careful consideration of relevant data is imperative
   before the procedures most conducive to effecting
   a desirable outcome can be determined.

Have you finished the exercise? Maybe that's the wrong question to ask. You don't really finish an exercise like this; you *abandon* it! Here are revisions you can compare with your own versions:

a. Number the samples as follows:

(The original sentence is periodic, wordy, contains an *ion* noun, and ends in passive voice. The revision starts with an active verb and wastes no words. If it were necessary to include the info on "to facilitate the identification of," the sentence could read,

"Number the samples as follows to make them easier to identify:")

b. The service company charges $4000 monthly for computer time, printouts, and system maintenance.

(Here's an example of non-parallel structure. In the original, "computer time" and "printed output" are nouns; "to maintain the system" is a verb form [prepositional phrase]. The revision changes each item to a noun. Did you note, too, that "is assessed by" is passive?)

c. I'll put all the firm's resources to work to make money for you.

(The original — 29 words — was written by a former stockbroker, now a waiter, attempting to assure a client of his firm's capabilities. The length, the stilted phraseology, and the vagueness conspire to impede understanding. The revision implies no promises, but straightforwardly states the broker's commitment.)

d. We must:
   · Remove phosphates from waste
   · Devise a way to detect oil spills early
   · Enact laws to prohibit industrial waste dumping

(The 29-word original was written by a legislative analyst. As in example *b*, the elements are non-parallel. "To remove" and "devising" are verb forms [infinitive and participle, respectively], while "creation" is a noun. "Must be taken" is passive, begging the question, "By whom?" The revision lists the action points, beginning each with an active-voice verb, and assigns responsibility ["We"].)

e. The program isn't paying off because we approve so few
    applications.

    (Written by a data processing technician, the original shoots
    itself in the foot: long [37 words], periodic, passive ["has been
    realized"], and difficult to follow. Just what does the buzz
    phrase "economically feasible" mean? The revision is concise,
    conversational, active, and direct.)

f. Look before you leap. Or, Think before acting.

    (Isn't either statement all the original actually says?)

When checking your revisions against mine, keep in mind that
these exercises represent "somebody else's" writing. Whenever you
supervise, you'll find yourself many times in the position of
reviewing other people's messages. And, while it's usually more fun
to critique somebody else's writing rather than our own, I'm trying
to get you to develop standards you'll apply to your own message
sending, too.

Remember to maintain a consistent *Tone* throughout your message.
I read and listen to far too many communications in which the sender
starts out like gangbusters, paying attention to familiar language,
active voice, sentences which are short and loose, and variety. But
then, halfway through, passive voice and long, periodic sentences
take over. The signal coming at me is one of sloppiness and laziness.
If you don't seem to care, why should your audience? Face it: our
messages convey infectious, contagious qualities. If you become
energetic and enthusiastic, these qualities will show up in your
communications and pass along to your audience. But if you fall flat,
your message can nosedive.

The following pointers for composing clearer sentences
supplement this chapter's discussion in helping you choose the
better way of getting your ideas across:

■ *Get rid of excess words —*

    Much business writing is full of words and phrases adding
    nothing to the meaning of a sentence. For example:

"I am writing to inform you that a
committee meeting is scheduled
for Friday."

The writing is obviously "writing to inform." Here's how
to streamline the sentence:

"The committee will meet Friday."

■ *Avoid starting sentences with "it" or "there" —*

These words are vague and weaken a sentence when
used at the beginning.

Instead of: "It is our intention to . . . ."
             "There are five managers meeting."

Write: "We intend . . . "
             "Five managers are meeting."

■ *Limit sentences to one main idea —*

Rather than cramming ideas like this:

"The meeting dates scheduled for the year are
listed below to permit you to submit to your
representative, through the vice president of
your division, any questions or other matters
you believe should be considered by the
committee."

Break up the points as separate ideas:

"The meeting dates for the year are listed below.
If you have questions for the committee, submit
them to your division vice president. He will
forward them to your committee representative."

Chapter 3 Review

Here are the main points to keep in mind from this chapter:

☞   Practice applying ingredients of **Message
      Mechanics** to establish the appropriate
      Tone of your communication and to
      generate interest — both for you and
      your audience.

☞   Keep the language level familiar.
      Avoid noun overuse and prefer verbs.

☞   Decide whether the active or passive
      voice — or a mix — is preferable.
      Remember that a considerable number
      of business communications suffer from
      excessive passive voice.

☞   Maintain a short, loose sentence style.
      Be concise, economical, and direct
      (as appropriate).

☞   Vary your use of **Message Mechanics**
      ingredients to avoid monotony and interject
      change of pace in your messages.

"Of all the arts at which the wise excel,
nature's chief masterpiece is writing well."
        – John Sheffield, 17th Century

Overview

This chapter discusses the second and third structural elements common to business messages: the *Opening* and the *Body*. We're now ready to move from the pre-composition to the composition stage. In doing so, the emphasis shifts from *process* to *product*. I'm not going to abandon the concepts presented so far. Rather, the intent is to build upon them.

This chapter presents categories to choose from when grappling with your introductory comments, and goes into detail on **Content Mapping** techniques. All the approaches are designed to help you further organize your thoughts in developing the most appropriate strategy for making informed choices.

> ## Structural Element Number
> ## Two: Opening – Where to Begin

The introduction of your message is the part the audience first sees or hears. That doesn't necessarily mean, though, that the *Opening* is the first part of the message you must wrangle with. Many workshop attendees have told me over the years that the introductory comments are the part of the message causing the most hassle. The opening often presents the highest preparation hurdle. What you're bumping up against if this happens to you is the old *getting motivated to get started* syndrome. The temptation to procrastinate is difficult to resist. In fact, it's not so much that you're unable to get started, but far more likely that you've decided (at least subconsciously) other things are worth doing. Make the message a priority.

Start At the Start?

Another concern at this stage is getting locked into thinking you must start preparing the actual text of a message at the beginning. Not true. No rule states you have to get going with the opening. After all, who but you has to see your first draft?

My advice is to look over your outline, then decide where you feel most comfortable about plunging in to compose your message, where you see a point of entry. It might be the *Body*. Or you may have a workable *Closing* statement formulated. So begin there. I've found it particularly helpful, for just about every kind of message, to compose the closing first, then work my way back through the document. This means I *reverse engineer* my thinking process and compose the middle of my presentation after my conclusion.

Finally, I'm prepared to develop *Opening* comments that tie in more tightly to the *Body* and the *Closing*. What does this process enable me to do? Provide a pathway through the communication for me and my audience, one that rounds out my idea flow, helping me attain a "full circle" approach (especially for <u>Action</u> messages).

Essentially, I'm asking you to consider what your ultimate destination is before you start the reader or listener off. This way you can better map out your strategy and the points you want to make along the way.

"Your Eyes Are the Color of My New Maserati"

No, I'm not going to provide you with a list of suggested great opening lines for your messages. If I did, I'd be doing your thinking for you. And, besides, any such list is bound to grow stale in a short time. Remember, you want to maintain variety in your style, particularly when communicating frequently with the same people. I can, though, provide you with suggestions. Keep in mind, first, that the wording in your *Opening* statements will very likely change from message to message. (Exceptions are form letters, and even they should be revised at least annually.)

When the wording stays the same, we slip into the rut of using interchangeable phraseology like "Enclosed please find," "As per your request," "We are in receipt of," and similar deadwood. It's gotten to the point in corporate America where most of our documents read and sound so alike that differentiating individual identities is nearly impossible.

Second, even though the word choice will vary, you'll have two constants — two categories, that is — into which you can slot your opening comments: **Emphatic** and **Low-key.**   By definition, an Emphatic opening is one which:

* Gets attention
* Conveys impact
* Is best used in <u>Action</u> messages

A Low-key opening has these hallmarks:

* Tends to give background first
* Is soft-sell in nature
* Is best used in <u>Information only</u> messages

Certainly, some crossing over may occur when choosing between these categories. By that I mean, you may find an *Emphatic* opening appropriate for an <u>Information only</u> message, or you may choose a *Low-key* opening for an <u>Action</u> document. You'll make the most suitable choice once you've clearly defined your objective and completed your audience profile.

Real-World Considerations

Let's examine the following memo opening and then go on to compare *Emphatic* and *Low-key* opening statements:

"This foremen's seminar proposes to present some
concepts of psychological understanding and then to
formulate a methodology for applying those concepts
to job-related issues."

Written by an industrial psychologist in a Human Resources department, the opening statement is, I'm sure, well-intended. But it's going to shop foremen, who are going to read it as mumbo-jumbo. Here's another pass:

"This foreman's seminar will show you how to handle
problems that come up on the job. For instance, you'll learn
how to deal with employees who are so sore about not getting
promoted that they don't turn in a full day's work. And

*you'll find out how to make peace between stockmen
whose bickering holds up production."*

Sure, the revision is longer. But it's *better.* It gives the audience members information they can use. One of the most significant bits of advice I can pass along to help you with your opening statements is to consider what people wonder when they first encounter your message. They want to know, "What is this about?" You need to tell them, to state your <u>purpose</u>, and to state it soon, simply, and succinctly. Here are examples of *Emphatic* and *Low-key* openings that help set a clear perspective:

Emphatic	Low-Ley
1. We're pleased to announce approval of your loan request.	1. After careful consideration, the loan committee has decided to approve your application.
2. Do you want to keep us as a customer?	2. I am writing for the third time to inform you of a problem we have in regard to shipment.
3. The company can save up to $60,000 annually by changing current reclaim practices.	3. If wasteful reclaim practices continue, the company could experience substantial losses (up to $60,000) annually.
4. We recommend withdrawing from the project because we found only traces of uranium.	4. A core sample was taken on a Jurassic rock slope. Groundwater flow was found along with variegated limestone strata. Inadequate uranium deposits were located to warrant further excavation.

Notice that the Emphatic version of each set is not only more concise than the Low-key counterpart, but is easier to understand. In addition, the focus for the audience on the message content is more sharply defined. Let's examine each set to analyze specifics:

1. The Low-key rendition was written by a savings & loan officer to a customer. Doesn't it imply, haughtily, that the applicant barely qualifies? It almost reads as though it's going to be a turndown. The Emphatic wording imparts a warmer customer-relations tone.

2. Look closely at the verbiage contained in the Low-key opening. The writer doesn't need "I am writing" (if he or she weren't, there'd be nothing to read). "In regard to" is superfluous. And what happened with the first two correspondences? Did they fall on blind eyes? I wonder when the sender expects to be taken seriously. With the fourth letter, or the fifth? The Emphatic version hits the reader between the eyes. Its tone is no-nonsense. If I received a message with that opening, I'd pay immediate attention. Which is the point. In fact, if the "shipment problem" is serious enough, the writer would be better off calling rather than writing to get a solution.

3. Here's an example of a Low-key opening bordering on the Emphatic because its tone is alarmingly negative. It led off a management briefing. The sentence is periodic, but the entire thought can leave a sour taste in the audience's mouth. Note the red-flag word "wasteful." It's preferable not to tell management that practices are wasteful — even if they are. The Emphatic version does a little somersault, turning the potential loss into a potential savings. It's a matter of communicating whether the glass is half-full or half-empty. Note, too, the substitution of "current" for "wasteful." No judgment is made now. Rather, a non-critical, neutral note is struck.

4. A bit of background will be helpful here. Mining engineers in Denver, Colorado, were hired by an East Coast oil company to conduct soil samples in the Rocky Mountains. The engineers completed their field work, then made an oral presentation for senior management. The Low-key opening doesn't present a context; it just starts reciting methodology. Note that each verb is passive. I have a "So what?" reaction to the first two points. The third sentence tells the

listeners what they need to know, but only at the very end of the paragraph. Its placement suggests the speaker is afraid of presenting this news. Buffers are fine, but not when they pussyfoot!

The Emphatic version, on the other hand, states action and pulls the key finding from the back to the front. Actually, it presents good news because now the client can stop pumping money down a dry hole, cut losses, take a tax write off, and explore for uranium elsewhere. The methodology about the core sample, the ground water, etc., may be important to convey, but put it after the more significant data.

The audience profile was awry in this example. Had the Low-key rendering been targeted toward geologists in the oil company, I'd say it was appropriate. But the senior managers at the presentation were MBA's, pursestring-pullers who occupy Mahogany Row. Their primary concerns are — if you'll pardon the trite expression — "bottom line." In such cases, use an Emphatic opening.

Sometimes Low-key wording can be so toned-down as to be underwhelming to read or listen to. For example, during the opening moments of an oral presentation I sat in on recently, the speaker was so low-key, so uninspiring, that I doubt whether the audience had any faith in her ability to energize her presentation. Because she mumbled and seemed disorganized, I felt like passing around No-Doz; I could see listeners ready to nod off. Her style was a yawner with only vague comments about the subject of her talk. In fact, she said so little of substance during the first five or ten minutes that I wondered when she was finally going to get around to the central idea, which I knew had to do with streamlining design methods. Give your audiences important points soon. And do so *emphatically*.

Results Occur As a Result of Effort

Too often, our tendency as message senders is to put the cart before the horse. By this I mean that we confuse efforts with results. On the job, we're getting paid for results, not just efforts. Without a doubt, efforts lead to results. Burning the midnight oil, working 60-hour weeks, are sometimes necessary, even admirable activities. But if they don't result in desired ends, they're wasted efforts. Results are paramount, and that's what we should be reporting. The

4th example on page 74 shows a classic case of this confusion: the first two points made in the *Low-key* version contain efforts. Better to locate secondary information like this in appendices, addendums or exhibits — at any rate, someplace other than in the opening.

Time again to test your ability to put into effect the principles being discussed. So take pen in hand and revise the following opening sentences. Where they are *Low-key,* try making them *Emphatic.* If they seem *Emphatic* enough, concentrate on **Message Mechanics** to reinforce what you learned from the previous chapter. Remember, there are no right or wrong answers. I'll offer suggested revisions and commentary once you've re-written these opening statements:

1. Consumer demand is falling in the area of service.

2. The Senior Engineer made a negative decision as to the development of the rotary bulk loader.

3. For the purpose of this experiment, we made use of a new analytical method.

4. A report giving the results of the work is in the process of preparation.

5. Throughout the whole of the Mesozoic Era, these rocks were affected by pressures from above.

6. It is the recommendation of this committee that steps be taken to ascertain the economic value of the ore body.

My suggested revisions:

1. Consumer service demand is falling.

(Get rid of "in the area of," and make "service" an adjective rather than a noun.)

2. The Senior Engineer decided not to develop the rotary bulk loader.

(Note that the original sentence could just as easily be interpreted to mean that the rotary bulk loader is going to be developed, but that the Senior Engineer made some kind of "negative decision" about it. Depending on sender intent and audience profile, these first two openings could be deemed *Emphatic.*)

3. We used a new analytical method for this experiment.

(The original is a wordy, periodic sentence. The revision cuts "the purpose of." I'd call this opening *Low-key.*)

4. We're preparing a report.

(Note the verbiage, the "ion" noun, and the passive voice in the original. The concise revision, which could be either *Emphatic* or *Low-key*, establishes a doer: We.)

5. Surface pressures affected these rocks throughout the Mesozoic era.

(The revision is a short, loose sentence from a *Low-key* opening. Don't substitute "during" for "throughout the whole of"; the meanings are different.)

6. The committee recommends assaying the ore.

(This *Emphatic* opening was wordy, passive, periodic, and vague. Granted, the revision contains a highly specific participle ["assaying"], but sometimes a precise word is required, even though it might drive the audience to the dictionary.)

Let's go back to our hypothetical IBM P/S 2 memo for a moment. At this first-draft stage, the preliminary wording for the opening is, "The purpose of this memo is to discuss the IBM P/S 2." That may not be our final draft, but at this point we've at least provided an intoduction to the message. We've gotten the wheels turning. The audience has a clear idea of what the message is about and what the objective is. So let's turn our attention to the third structural item common to any communication, the **Body.**

**Structural Element Number
Three: Body – Communication
Crux**

This is the heart of your message, where you're presenting the most detail, the documentation and substantiation supporting your findings or conclusions. It typically takes up — more than the other structural elements — the most physical space. For instance, the middle is usually somewhere between 50% and 75% of your message. Compare that with the beginning and end, which seldom account for more than 25% of the message each. So, there's much information to manage in the *Body*.

Forgetfulness Factor

Unfortunately, this is the part of the communication the audience is most likely to forget first. It doesn't normally convey the same impact or impression as the *Opening* or *Closing*.   In fact, psychological research demonstrates that people remember first what they read or hear last. Next, they tend to remember the first part of a message. A "forgetfulness factor" affects what comes in between. Too often, that's because the *Body* is forgettable.

How can you minimize the tendency to "lose" the body, to give it a dynamic, memorable quality instead?   Well, you need to keep applying the steps this book has discussed so far. In addition, you'll find a great deal of help by using **Content Mapping** techniques when composing or delivering information in the body of any message.

These techniques assist in giving form and coherence to the body, eliminating rambling or disjointed idea presentation. Since the body has such significance, I'm going to spend more time on it than on the other structural elements.   Here's what **Content Mapping** is comprised of:

1. *Using Signposts—* An apt analogy here is to imagine setting out on a journey of considerable distance, especially one taking you into new or unfamiliar territory. You wouldn't just pull the Ferrari out

of the garage without the slightest idea of where you wanted to go, would you? (Ah, yes, New York to San Francisco.) Planning a route will not only help you "map out" the major destinations you hope to arrive at, but will aid in negotiating your way along the journey. Your role is that of guide.

Imagine having to fend for yourself on an African safari. You'd feel better going along with someone who's been there before, who knows the terrain. Think along these lines when you're composing the *Body* of any communication. Don't just turn the audience loose to make their own way. They may get sidetracked. Rather, take them by the hand and lead them along. They'll be grateful for receiving direction and support.

Reader Clues

If I were traveling along a roadway without signs to guide me, I'd find it difficult getting my bearings, anticipating turns, reroutes, exits, and so on. Headings used in the *Body* of your message act as highway signposts, clueing the audience to what's coming up and helping to propel your readers or listeners through the message. (Try to imagine the L.A. freeways without road signs. They'd be chaotic. Come to think of it, those freeways are *already* chaotic. Without signs, they'd be *utterly* chaotic.)

Headings Preview Content

Use headings, then, as signposts taken from your outline, which you'll probably find you expand upon to accommodate increasing levels of detail. For example, look over the following paragraph from a technical user manual:

> "*Your first option on the Design Module Main Menu deals with point/curve creation. Within this function you will create most types of geometric entities. Examples of Multigraphics geometric entities include points, lines, and arcs.*"

As you read the paragraph, you naturally wonder what it's about. The outline point — or "spoke" — probably indicated "points and curves," which is okay for an outline, but rather static for a final document. But if you first see the heading, CREATING POINTS AND CURVES, the information is activated. You can keep in mind what the topic is and arrive sooner at a more comprehensive understanding. Here are some examples of headings which introduce paragraphs in the body of a report:

Business Activity

Sales volumes and earnings levels for the past 12 months registered healthy gains for a majority of firms. Expectations for the next 3 years are equally favorable. Increases in inventories and accounts receivable will accompany the higher projected sales volumes.

Inflation

Rising inflation did not significantly impact most company profit margins. The bulk of inflationary costs are evidently passed to the customer and the ultimate consumer. No one is forecasting a nationwide recession during the next year.

Projected Trends

Profitability and productivity will increase for most major corporations. Growth stimulation will result directly from new capital investment and limited government regulation. Employees of these targeted operations will benefit from predicted job security and stability.

Now, suppose these paragraphs had no headings and you were reading them to get information about inflation. You'd have to read each paragraph and make mental notes as you did so. But the heading Inflation is a courtesy the writer provides. It lets you zero in on the topic and skip what's not pertinent. The heading also allows the message sender, in the first place, to corral his or her thoughts — to *organize* the message. For example, the writer might notice that a first draft contains inflation information in the first and second paragraphs. But the heading use enables moving the data to its appropriate location. Which brings up something they *did* teach us in school, or tried to, at least: topic sentences.

One Topic Per Paragraph

Remember Miss Thistlebottom telling you paragraphs contain a topic sentence and one or more developmental sentences? You don't? Well, that's less to unlearn, then. Even if you do remember, the lesson is more technical than it has to be. Headings indicate topics. They focus attention — for you and your audience — on what's being discussed. It's evident how headings, or signposts, work in written communications. When you're speaking, you can easily use the same technique by saying "My next topic is," or some similar wording.

You'll note that the three example paragraphs on page 81 each contain short, loose sentences with active-voice verbs. I'll have more to say about them shortly.

You may wonder, "Does every paragraph need a heading?" Not necessarily. In the report from which the preceding sample paragraphs were taken, the section on <u>Inflation</u> contained four paragraphs, but only one heading. As you proceed from topic to topic you can provide a consideration to your audience by labeling the topic changes appropriately. To illustrate: You may have a broad subject-matter heading and a series of subheadings — each signaling a new topic — under that broad subject, like so:

SYSTEM PARAMETERS

– Grid On/Off

– Display Grid

By labeling the changes you provide a consideration to your audience.

[Obiter dicta: I generally recommend using the participle (the "ing" suffix) when composing signposts: **Getting Started** instead of **How to Get Started**. At times, however, for the sake of variety, or when other wording is more descriptive, the participle isn't necessary.]

2.) *Establishing Idea Flow*— The signpost technique leads directly to setting up a flow of ideas, usually in list form, to show relational continuity among the points you're making in the body. Once you align topic points suggested by your outline, you're next ready to decide on their sequence or "firing order." You may decide not to deliver a prose narrative paragraph to best convey point discussion, but to itemize vertically, as shown here:

> *Use the CALCULATOR function as follows :*
> *∗ Enter a register reference letter*
> *∗ Follow it with an equal (=) sign*
> *∗ Press 'ENTRY'*

Main Points First

This technique is especially well-suited to composing step-by-step instructions or procedures, when your objective is to educate the audience about a specific process. Note that each of the listed points in the previous example begins with an action verb. It's helpful to arrange your thoughts by priority ranking within the firing order you've established, giving main points first, then secondary or less important points as you continue. Setting up a segmental flow assists in keeping your discussion "top heavy"; i.e., first presenting information that's critical to absorb, followed by the next set of significant data.

Bullets

When listing, use a bullet (∙) to signal each point rather than a number or a letter, *unless* you're deliberately indicating serial presentation or weighting certain points. The example under #2 above of vertically itemized points uses asterisks as bullets. In fact, you'll note that a number of my entries throughout this book do the same. (See page x at the back of the book for more information .)

3. *Composing Unified Paragraphs* — Just what is a paragraph, anyway? A bunch of sentences? Here's an English handbook definition: A paragraph is a set of related thoughts. Stray thoughts can impede understandability, so link together all the sentences within each of your paragraphs. Here's where signposts assist not only the message receiver but you, the sender.

With **Content Mapping**, paragraphs usually demonstrate two hallmarks. First, they're unified (another lesson Miss Thistlebottom imparted), meaning all the sentences deal with the same topic. And second, the paragraphs contain from 1 to 4 sentences, with bite–size, reader–friendly chunks of information.   This count is completely arbitrary on my part, because, according to the rules of language, a paragraph has no fixed length. But I'm offering the suggested range for the following reason:

Our organization is undertaking a concerted effort to determine how to and implement ways to maintain total workload manageability at the same time we meet our internal quarterly objectives and satisfy customer concerns and/or expectations. To this end, directives have been issued requiring optimal strategic planning become a measurable part of any and all performance evaluations scheduled to be conducted in the short term. As managers, an effort to assure compliance with their criteria, to ensure coordination, cooperation and continuation of ongoing activity is critical. This report sets forth guidelines to be adhered to pertaining to the performance evaluation process. They represent considerable, significant addenda to the current performance evaluation process, which they supersede.

Dense paragraphs like this are one of the biggest communication dealkillers, inducing MEGO (my eyes glaze over) faster than prescription sleep medications. Keep your paragraphs bite size, or you lock readers and listeners out.

Idea Dump

Simply "idea dump" your first draft. Don't worry about trying to get everything right or to compose letter–perfect paragraphs. (Again: Who else but you has to see your first draft?) Besides, critically judging every word as you write inhibits the message–sending process.   And try to resist the tendency to edit as you compose.   Your initial task is to get the ideas out of your head and onto paper or the word processing screen. For example, the following paragraph might represent your first–draft attempt:

"Masking (discussed in the next lesson) uses alternate
action from the Class Selection Menu to mask or filter the
types of entities that can be selected. Although an
optional step because a mask is not always required,
a mask can be set allowing arc and line selection only,
because no other 'masked' entities can be selected
from the selection process."

You can check the points for coherence (understandability) by referring to the **Message Mechanics** discussed in detail in Chapter 2. If the sentences cram ideas together, look for ways to effectively bridge the thoughts by using transitions such as these common ones:

however	on the other hand	yet
furthermore	similarly	but
thus	in conclusion	likewise
because	finally	although
therefore	moreover	since

Here's a revision to the above paragraph using what's been discussed so far:

MASKING

You can mask (or filter) the types of selected entities by using
Alternate Action from the Class Selection Menu. For instance,
you can set a mask allowing you to select only arcs and lines.
This setting eliminates other entities masked from the selection
process. Since a mask is not always required, this step is
optional. (See the next lesson for a further discussion.)

Note that the revision contains this tracking mechanism:

* Heading (signpost)
* Short, loose sentences with thoughts unified
* Personalized tone (second–person "you" used)
* Active voice preferred

With practice, your revisions can be as readily — and as simply — accomplished. Which means you polish your style as you proceed.

Paragraph Type

Like sentences, paragraphs can also be <u>loose</u> (main idea up front) or <u>periodic</u> (main idea at end). Determine which category your first draft of a paragraph comes under. To help gain a perspective, let's return to the IBM Personal System 2 memo we began putting together earlier. Here are examples of the types of paragraphs likely to be in the *Body*:

<u>Loose Paragraph</u>

"*Each month, our department can achieve a savings increase of about $12,000 and a productivity boost of 5%. The IBM Personal System 2 can help us get these results by automating reference tasks and freeing staffers to concentrate on marketing duties. Each model unit (hardware & software) currently retails in the $2200–7500 range.*"

<u>Periodic Paragraph</u>

"*Purchasing the IBM Personal System 2 will cost up to $7500. The current retail price of each model unit (hardware & software) averages $4850. But the investment will pay dividends of automated reference tasks and more concentrated marketing activity. Cost is readily justified by these estimated monthly increases for the department:*

＊ $12,000 savings
＊ 5% productivity boost"

The <u>loose</u> paragraph dangles a carrot right away. The idea flow proceeds from benefits to pricing information. If you were trying to sell or motivate your audience, the loose paragraph would be preferable. Do you notice the ownership attitude it conveys?

The <u>periodic</u> paragraph is preferable if, for instance, you are asked to provide info on cost. This paragraph is the inverse of the loose version: it proceeds from pricing to benefits. The reader may tend to skim the first part of the paragraph (which is where topic sentences usually come) and may not get to the selling points.

Is one type of paragraph better than the other? Not necessarily. Better to ask whether one is more efficient. Since people tend to remember first what they read last, the <u>periodic</u> version above *may* be the more efficient choice. It lists benefits at the end, making them stand out. The <u>loose</u> version, though, gets to the significant points right away, provided you determine that's what the audience needs to know.

Thought Sequence

Look back at the example paragraphs on page 81. In addition to being concise and containing headings, each has only three, under-20-word sentences. Note, too, the sequence of the idea flow in each. It's chronological. The first two paragraphs proceed from past to present to future. (Check the verb tenses.) In the third paragraph, each verb is future tense, begging the question, "Must every paragraph be chronological, containing past, present, and future info?" No. But that's one of the ways of sorting out thoughts and making them easier to follow. I try to apply the chronology where possible, either within paragraphs, or from one to the next. Sometimes I'll start off with future information and then go on to present or past.

Other ways of establishing thought sequence are to arrange ideas in order of importance; in deductive (general-to-specific) or inductive (specific-to-general) order; by geographical location (for example, activity in the Denver, Houston, and New Orleans offices); or by simple topic separations, which may not be in any particular order. What's important is that the *unit of thought* makes sense to the audience.

Try to avoid mixing verb tenses within paragraphs. For example, don't start off with past tense, go on to present or future, and then return to past without indicating a break. Lump all the past, present, and future information together. Not doing so creates what I call the *tennis-match syndrome.* The audience gets whipsawed back and forth, like trying to follow a tennis ball in play, losing all track of sequence. The following paragraph gives you an example of the *tennis-match syndrome* (the numbers indicate line count):

"*Since the warning letter was as effective as the preliminary*
2   *hearing and required less time, we believe a warning letter*
     program should be initiated. Because the preliminary
4   *hearing appeared to reduce accidents in selected rural areas*
     of the state, we feel preliminary hearings should be
6   *conducted to the extent possible outside urban areas and*
     warning letters should be issued to drivers who cannot be
8   *readily contacted for a hearing. We also recommend that*
     further evaluations of preliminary hearings in rural
10   *communities be conducted."*

Let's examine the mechanical and content problems:

A) The first sentence contains 24 words; the second, 45. Plus, each sentence is periodic.

B) The paragraph is overloaded with passive voice. (Line 3, "should be initiated"; Lines 5–6, "should be conducted"; Line 7, "should be issued"; Lines 7–8, "cannot be contacted"; Line 10, "be conducted.")

C) The vocabulary is inconsistent. On Line 2 the writer uses "believe," on Line 5 "feel," and on Line 8 "recommend." The words don't mean the same thing. "Recommend" is the strongest and clearest verb. (Incidentally, I recommend not using "feel" in business communications because you're not dealing with feelings in these kinds of messages. You're dealing with thoughts and ideas. Save "feel" for personal messages, such as, "Dear Mom, I feel Dad should put my name back in the will.") "Should" — used three times in the paragraph — is tentative and conditional. Its indefiniteness lets the audience off; they're not being told what must be done.

D) The paragraph is dense, not reader-friendly. Rather, it's style is off-putting. Plus, the thoughts are rambling and disjointed. While only three sentences long, the paragraph doesn't focus the reader's attention on a defined topic. You wonder what it's about and what its benefits are.

Now, let me give you some context. This is a paragraph taken at random from an investigative report to recommend ways of reducing highway accidents. It went to a state department of transportation. Now that you know more about diagnosing the inherent problems and what the information is supposed to convey, take a few minutes to try your hand at a revision. Here's what I'd like you to do:

- Give the information a subject or
  topic <u>heading</u>

- Make the sentences <u>loose</u> and the
  passive voice <u>active</u>

- List the recommendations

- State benefits

Check how you did against this revision, which applies **Message Mechanics** and **Content Mapping** techniques:

Accident Reduction Program

The warning letter was as effective as the preliminary hearing and required less time. Additionally, the hearing appeared to reduce accidents in selected rural areas. Therefore, we recommend these steps:

- *Initiate a warning letter program.*
- *Conduct preliminary hearings where possible.*
- *Issue warning letters to drivers not
  contacted for hearings.*
- *Evaluate further the effects of
  preliminary hearings in rural communities.*

Putting these recommendations into effect will benefit the state because reducing accidents will save lives.

Quite a dramatic difference, isn't it? Note that:

-The sentences are concise and manageable
-All the background is lumped together in the first two sentences
-The transition "Therefore" leads into the recommendations
-"Believe," "feel," and "should" are eliminated
-The steps begin with active-voice verbs
-The last statement comes full circle, linking the idea of

reducing accidents with positive, beneficial information.

Adding Audience Incentive

At the same time you use **Content Mapping** to make the message coherent in the *Body*, keep in mind the audience. What stimulus or impetus are you giving them to respond favorably? Here's where *benefits* play a highly significant role.

When you began organizing your message, you'll recall that one of my suggested steps was to dig to find benefits for your readers or listeners. To review broadly, I indicated that benefits usually involve such concerns as showing the audience how to save time or money, how to boost productivity by putting people to better use, or how to make more effective decisions. (Remember, these are by no means the only benefit categories; you'll undoubtedly think of specific others for your various messages.)

The Accident Reduction Program revision sample above concludes with a benefit statement. It points out the payback — gives a rationale — for putting recommendations into effect. In fact, if we "x-ray" the sample, so to speak, we find an information framework proceeding from *findings* to *recommendations* to *benefits*. Typically, this methodology works well for sections of report or presentation bodies. You can even apply it to paragraphs within those sections.

Often, successfully written bodies of Audit reports present item discussions that include Findings and Recommendations, with benefits tied to the specific action points. For example:

> * *ITEM: Lock boxes.*
>
> Finding — *Keys are not assigned to one clerk only, as required by Procedure 181.*
>
> Recommendation — *Assign keys only to the supervising lock-box clerk to ensure that unauthorized entries do not occur.*

Within the recommendation is a justification or a statement of "why" the report author is making the recommendation. You'll find benefits critical any time you're preparing an <u>Action</u> message — one which attempts to change the audience's behavior.   An apt example is procedures writing.   Many business writers make the mistake of merely stating procedures imperatively (starting with action verbs in step–by–step lists) *without* telling the reader why the steps are to be taken. Now, I'm not saying that each procedural step requires an accompanying justification. Rather, put a benefit or "why" statement as an introductory lead–in to a set of procedures.   Here's an example from a Southern California aerospace firm:

TOOL WITHHOLD PROCEDURE

I. <u>PURPOSE</u>

This procedure establishes the method for Quality Assurance to handle defective tools.

II. <u>PROCEDURE</u>

Quality Assurance Inspector:

A. Determines when conditions warrant withholding tools.
B. Notifies the QA Inspection Supervisor of defective tools.
C. Enters all information specifically describing the defective tool on a Withhold Tag.
D. Describes action taken to resolve the withhold condition in the space provided on the Tag.
E. Obtains the QA Inspection Supervisor's signature for the Withhold Tag or imprints the Tag with a signature stamp.

Benefits = Rationale

Can you have action messages that don't contain benefits? Yes, but they're rare. Let's say, for instance, that you're composing a letter to a vendor, cancelling that vendor's contract at the end of the month. The action you're trying to get the reader to perform is to <u>not</u> continue providing services, to stop doing business with you.

Are there benefits to that reader? No. But he or she is due an explanation of *why* you're canceling the contract. Maybe it's because certain conditions of the service agreement are being disregarded, and attempts to rectify the situation have apparently fallen on deaf ears. Whatever your motivation for communicating, make sure you convey the reason to the audience.

When attempting to add incentive in the *Body*, remember that people tend to behave in terms of what satisfies their own self-interests. I mentioned the premise earlier in this book: People do things for *their* reasons, not yours. But, if you're an effective communicator, you're able to persuade or convince your audience members that their self-interests and yours converge, that you're on their side.

Very often, we're put off when having to send a message — written or oral — which we know isn't going to be favorably received. We become inhibited in our effectiveness because resistance to what we have to say or write is inevitable. These so-called "bad news" messages usually show much equivocating or pussyfooting on our part. But you can still be direct, even forceful, though you may not be able to win over an audience. I've given up on always trying to change peoples' minds when I communicate with them. Granted, there are times when I'm going to be able to do just that, when I can get people to rethink their point of view.

Support — Don't Defend — Your Ideas

But at the very least, I'm trying to demonstrate how I've arrived at my position, even if I'm taking a stand at odds with my audience. In other words, I want them to understand *why* I think as I do. The old saying that "If you don't stand for something, you'll stand for anything" is applicable here. If I'm an effective communicator, even though you may not go along with me, you'll understand — and respect — how I've arrived at my point of view. Here's where I stand, and by gosh, you have to give me credit for the basis of my convictions.

Just make sure that your arguments do hold up, that you present facts (distinguished from opinion), and that your message ultimately speaks for itself. For example, if I make this statement in a report:

Sales last month were good (or excellent, or other such adjective), I'm presenting opinion, and non-specific opinion at that. Nothing is wrong with presenting opinion in a message, but always ask yourself whether you can enhance the communication with factual data you can support, such as: *Sales last month exceeded projected expectations by 4%.* Note that this sales indicator is neither good nor bad; the audience can decide for itself whether the percentage excess is favorable or not.

Avoid the trap of trying to defend, rather than support, information presented in the *Body.* When you get defensive, it's easy for emotion to take over; by adopting a supportive tone, you let the facts speak for themselves, thus eliminating bias. Evaluate the psychological strategy of presenting the information this way: *We are pleased to report that sales last month exceeded projected expectations by 4%.*

When you're trying to "sell" the audience, go ahead and lean in the direction you've already arrived at, but be careful not to open yourself up to accusations of prejudicial message sending. Sometimes you can bail yourself out by stating openly that you're presenting opinion, or preliminary information. This way you distance yourself from the message (eliminate ownership) and introduce an element of objectivity, which may be greatly appreciated.

When Objectivity is Critical

In fact, objectivity is strictly called for in analytical or scientific documents when the aim is impersonality and impartiality. Here, what's called for is passive voice (but not excessively so), directness, professionalism, and *factual* presentation. For example, an attendee at one of my recent workshops was an investigator for the National Transportation Safety Board, one of the agencies immediately on the scene at airplane crashes. His job is to write investigative reports detailing how such crashes occur; the documents must not be speculative as to *why.*

My critique of his communication style revealed a simple vocabulary concern: too many conditional words like "may," "maybe," "perhaps," "might," "seems," "appears," "could" and the like. None of these words conveys conclusive factual information. I helped the investigator eliminate them from his analysis reports. To illustrate: here's a statement from an NTSB report critiqued during the workshop:

> *Pilot error may have caused the engine failure.*

The investigator revised this statement to:

> *Pilot error has not been ruled out as*
> *a cause of engine failure.*

The original statement presents opinion. The revision is factual — about the subject of continuing investigation, *not* about the cause of the engine failure.

[**Obiter Dicta:** Check for those times in your
own writing when a necessary distance is called
for between you and the message you're conveying.
But try to avoid the overly stilted third-person use
such as "the author (or writer)," "the undersigned,"
or "one"(as in "One must carefully consider . . . ").
Why refer to yourself in the third person,
particularly within the personal, familiar framework
of letters and memos?]

Chapter 4 Review

Keep in mind these significant points about composition:

☞ Remember that the *Body* takes up the most
physical space in the message. It's the heart
of what you're communicating and the
information the audience is most likely
to forget.

☞ **Content Mapping** techniques help to organize
and lend coherence to your message. They are
made up of:
- Using Signposts
- Establishing Idea Flow
- Composing Unified Paragraphs

☞ Simply "idea dump" your first drafts. You'll revise them by pouring them into the **Message Mechanics** and **Content Mapping** molds.

☞ Add audience incentive by spelling out *benefits.*

"It ain't over till it's over."
                    – Anonymous

Overview

The conclusion of the message is your final point of impact with the audience. Three categories of *Closing* statements will help slot your thoughts appropriately for readers or listeners. Most important for <u>Action</u> messages is to bring thoughts full circle, to satisfyingly "round out" the communication.

+---+
| |
| **Structural Element Number** |
| **Four: Closing – The Final** |
| **Curtain** |
| |
+---+

Inefficiently prepared communications either fall off the end of the page when written, or drift off into space when spoken. I tend to see too many boilerplate statements like this at the end of letters or memos: *"Please do not hesitate to contact me if I can be of any further assistance in this matter."* It's come to substitute for a closing in most written corporate or government communications. As a courtesy statement, all it really says is that the writer is alive and breathing should the reader need to get in touch. But it fails to efficiently close out the message.

We use the same old wording far too frequently in letters and memos, but tend to grope for effective conclusions when speaking, stammering feebly ("Uh, okay then . . . any questions?") instead of wrapping up forcefully and conclusively. Often, the tendency is to repeat unnecessarily something from an earlier part of the message rather than deliberately drive home key information. That's true whether we're speaking or writing. Look at the diagram that follows at the top of the next page:

* Your objective/reaction
* Reinforce [letters, memos]
         or
Summarize [reports, presentations]

Here's what this figure suggests remembering when you're ready to compose concluding comments:

√ Remind yourself of the objective you had in mind when you began preparing the message two hours ago or two days ago (or however long it might be). You'll recall from Chapter 1 that step #1 in *Organize the Message* is to define your objective (see page 12); step #5 is to decide what reaction you want (see page 24). The *Closing* is where you'll come to grips with that reaction, so make sure it's specific.

For example, audience members can't help but wonder, as you finish your communication, "What happens next?" Tell them. Will you, the message sender, be taking followup responsibility? Must the reader or listener do anything? Is *anything* to be done? Let your audience know where to go from here if you're presenting an <u>Action</u> message.

√ Repeat (by *reinforcing* or *summarizing*) a key point or points from earlier in the message to make sure the information registers with your audience. Be certain that what you reinforce or summarize is significant for your reader or listener. [Review question #2 from *Assessing Your Audience*, Chapter 2, page 33.] Don't merely run out of ideas and let the closing sputter and fizzle or, just as inefficient, *needlessly* repeat insignificant data.

For instance, I once received a letter from an accountant which opened with a "thank you" for taking him out to lunch. He then went on to discuss some of my estimated tax liabilities. His closing contained another "thank you" for the delightful lunch. I was much more concerned about the amount I owed the IRS!   My point is, he didn't need to thank me twice for buying lunch (which, it turned out, I was able to write off).   But I'm sure he simply didn't know how to end the letter and just doubled back around to the opening.   I remember rereading the body of that message to understand what I had to do by April 15. Had the writer reinforced that action in the closing, the information would have had greater impact.

If you're looking for something to double back around to from the *Opening* or the *Body*, concentrate on:

>   – *Findings*
>   – *Recommendations*
>   – *Benefits*

Typically, the closing is where you'll locate action points such as recommendations.   But you may have presented them earlier, as was the case in the *tennis-match syndrome* revision (see Chapter 4, page 89).   You can make a general statement in the closing about recommendations which might be specifically located in the body. Audit reports, for example, don't usually lump all recommendations together at the end of the document, but present them incrementally throughout body discussion (linked with benefits).

Don't Try This at Work

Let's look at an example of how *not* to write a closing. The letter request that follows was an attempt to get <u>Action</u>. It failed miserably. As you read it, analyze each of the other three structural elements, too, to see where the writer might have improved.   While I'd like you to concentrate on how to make the *Closing* more effective, getting an *overall* idea of why the message doesn't work will be helpful.

Failed Message:

>   *John Marshall*
>   *Eby & Everson*
>   *1300 Grant*
>   *Denver, CO*   <u>*RE*</u>*: Payne Expedition*

Dear John:

I need your help!

I've sent factsheets to ABC, CBS, and NBC in New York, suggesting that the Payne Expedition is a national project worthy of some type of network coverage.

To date, I've received no reply. Maybe the material ended up in someone's wastebasket. I had no specific name or department to which I could send the factsheets, except for the ABC News Closeup feature.

Maybe you could use your influence to help us gain television exposure. As you mentioned the other day, you'd think the Payne Expedition would be a natural. Maybe we'll have to help it along.

I'd appreciate your giving it some thought, John, and then getting back in touch with me.

Ready to critique? Okay, let's start with this question: What's the writer's objective? Is it to get the names of contact people at the TV networks to publicize the Payne Expedition? (Which, incidentally, was a horseback ride from Denver to Washington, D.C., commemorating Colorado's statehood proclamation.) The writer never came right out and said, "I need the names of three contact people at the TV networks."

Audience Assessment

How about the reader profile? Let's say John Marshall runs an Advertising/PR firm in Denver. (We'll assume he has the necessary TV contacts.) What types of people run Ad/PR firms? Do you think the reader is a shy, withdrawn, Caspar Milquetoast type? Probably not. The profession demands a certain type of personality. Think of people you know who work in such firms. They're likely outgoing, creative, dynamic, *busy* people — the type who'll respond favorably to an *Emphatic Opening*, which the writer did use.

Pleading Attitude

In fact, I'd characterize the *Tone* (or attitude) of the opening as "desperate." I get an image of the writer down on bended knee. And that's fine. But is the tone maintained throughout the message? It isn't. The closing simply fizzles out. Note that the paragraphs are reader–friendly, and the sentences concise, with active voice. Only one sentence exceeds 20 words (the second), and could easily be shortened to two sentences. I'll also give the writer credit for his chronological idea flow in the body. But the vocabulary is weak and conditional. The word "maybe" is used three times. It seems the writer is backing away from the subject rather than dealing directly. I almost expect the closing to read, "Ah, forget it."

Something else is lacking in the body: *incentive.* What's in it for the reader to help out? Maybe the writer could have told John Marshall, "This will be a feather in your agency's cap if you'll do this for us," or "I'll return the favor by taking you to lunch at your favorite restaurant." Without incentive it's difficult to get audiences to go along.

Opening Up the Closing

The writer yanks the rug right out from under himself in the *Closing.* He certainly wants a reaction other than "some thought." And when, exactly, should the reader get back in touch? Whenever? How could the writer have "rounded out" the document? Well, the opening is effectively written. Why not reinforce the idea of needing help and *participate with the reader* in meeting the message objective. How? The answer leads me to a discussion of categories into which you can slot your closing thoughts.

Direct, Suggestive, Provocative

Any communication — written or oral — can close on a *Direct, Suggestive* or *Provocative* note, or a combination among them. I'll define each and give you examples, explaining in the process how the categories apply to the Payne Expedition letter:

■ *Direct* closings tell. They are authoritative and forthright. Use them with subordinates or peers, for the most part. Be careful how direct you are with superiors. Would it be wise to use, for example, this wording in a message to your company president: "You must respond in writing within three days"? Probably not. In fact, such wording may close out your career.

In the Payne Expedition letter, the writer simply dumped the problem in the reader's lap. He could have participated with the reader in a direct manner by wording the closing as: "I'll call you by the end of the week to get network contact names." In this version, the writer keeps the ball in his court, and indicates he'll take followup responsibility. Note the timeframe reference. This is a typical hallmark of a *Direct* closing.

Psychologists tell us that people tend to respond favorably to directives when we add a deadline. Just make sure your suggested response timeframe is reasonable. The writer in the sample letter could have told John Marshall to call him within a certain timeframe after he got the letter. Or he could have kept the ball in his court by indicating that he'd make followup contact.

■ *Suggestive* closings defer. "Defer" has two definitions: to postpone or to show politeness toward. If you want to leave the next move up to your audience, this category is appropriate. For example, instead of being direct with your company president, you could word the closing suggestively: "I'd appreciate a written response at your convenience." Note that this wording is declarative; conversely, the direct approach — when you *tell* the audience to do something — is imperative. (Would you categorize the closing in the sample memo on page 100 as Suggestive?)

■ *Provocative* closings ask. You end the message with a question. What's the value of doing so? I refer again to my source the behavioral psychologists, who say that when we ask questions — face-to-face, over the phone, or in writing — we create momentarily a state of tension in the reader's or listener's subconscious. People can't live with unresolved states of tension, so they'll answer the question, at least to themselves. If you think about it, I've been asking questions throughout this book, always in a subtle attempt to draw you into my narrative.

Remember when Miss Thistlebottom asked a question of your fourth-grade class, and you didn't have the answer? Most likely, you avoided eye contact with her, and you certainly didn't raise your hand. (One of my ploys to deflect attention was to hide behind the classmate who sat in front of me and pretend I was still studiously taking notes, oblivious to the question. It rarely worked.)

If, on the other hand, you did have the answer, you looked directly at the teacher, your hand shot into the air, and you were hoping to be called on. But, whether or not you had the answer, the question's being asked created the tension. Teachers — and effective communicators — ask questions to <u>provoke</u> responses, thus the label *Provocative*. Of course, you're hoping to get a positive reaction (no one wants to hear "No"). Much of that has to do with the way you phrase the question.

Check the wording to be sure you're on the right track. Take a lesson from the example of a meek door-to-door encyclopedia salesman who asked, once a prospective buyer opened the door, "You wouldn't want to buy a set of encyclopedias, would you?"

Don't set yourself up for defeat. The salesman would have been better off asking, "Would you like to ensure that your children get better marks in school?" (Remember the value of <u>benefits</u> when you're selling . . . or when generating an *Action* business communication.)

Drawing the Audience In

If you're familiar with computer-based training methodology, you know that the computer is programmed to ask questions as the learner proceeds. This process invites interaction and dispels passivity in education. Asking questions can take some of the edge off too direct an approach when closing a message, but provide more punch than being suggestive. For example, the letter to John Marshall could have ended provocatively: "Will you call me next week with contact names at the network?"

Here are four sample closing statements from various messages rendered as *Direct, Suggestive,* and *Provocative*:

Direct:

> I'll call you within a week.
> Take immediate steps to resolve these issues.
> Begin the conversion procedures by May 15.
> We must renew Stacon's line of credit.

Suggestive:

> Call me at your convenience.
> Consider taking steps to resolve these issues.
> You can begin the conversion procedures.
> We should renew Stacon's line of credit.

Provocative:

> May I please hear from you as soon as
> possible?
> Will you see that these issues are resolved?
> Can I expect you to begin the conversion
> procedures by May 15?
> Can we afford not to renew Stacon's line
> of credit?

The *Closing* can also be a longer recap:

Summary

Our findings are based on preliminary investigation. Not all the necessary data is available to determine conclusively the cause of the action that occurred during processing.

However, we recommend instituting a policy of control processes. We can eliminate confusion on the part of the temporary staff and establish a record of transactions to prevent similar occurrences.

You can see that some combining, some mixing & matching, is evident (the May 15 deadline in the third Provocative closing, for instance, adds a direct element). In the first Provocative closing, we could substitute "within a week" from the first Direct version for "as soon as possible." The hybrid "May I please hear from you within a week?"' now becomes a Direct–Provocative combination, increasing the chances of getting results.

Who's taking followup responsibility in the first Direct closing? The message sender. You can see that the next move is up to the receiver in the Suggestive rendering.

The second and third Direct closings start with action verbs; they're imperative. The sender is probably a boss and the receiver a subordinate. Note the open–ended quality as they become suggestive.

Honoring the Office Chain of Command

The final Direct closing was written by a bank trainee in a memo to officers. Is it politically wise for a trainee to use that *Tone*? The Suggestive revision may be preferable. "Should" in a closing statement equates with being Suggestive. I cautioned you earlier to be wary of "should" overuse. But you can by all means use the word to indicate deference. The trainee settled on the Provocative version for her memo. It comes at the objective from a different angle and reads like a breath of fresh air. Think of all that's unsaid though implied in the Provocative wording.

A summary in the closing can (but doesn't *have* to) distill findings, then recommendations and benefits, just as I've suggested doing in an executive summary or in sections of the body when writing **Action** reports. Am I implying that reports should contain an executive summary up front and a final summary at the end? Yes, I am. But make a judgment call. In a short report, a closing summary may be redundant. For a longer report, an opening summary previews and a closing summary recaps. Give it to them twice; that way the message is much more likely to register and generate a response. A concluding summary is absolutely critical at the end of a speech.

Part By Part, All Self–Contained

Keep in mind that each section of a lengthy document such as a report or a proposal can contain its own *Opening*, *Body*, and *Closing*, with consistent *Tone* threaded throughout. If a reader refers to nothing more than a particular portion of the document, you've at least given that section a stand–alone quality. And if you're really good, the part gives a flavor of the whole — a process known, by the way, as *synecdoche.*

Closing Applications

So how do you choose from the three categories of closings? Always first review your objective and audience profile. I classify *Direct* and *Provocative* closings as appropriate for **Action** messages. *Suggestive* closings work best for **Information only** communications. You'll recall I mentioned in Chapter 4, when discussing openings, that I often write my closing first, then work back, or "reverse engineer" from the end point through the body and into the opening.

The process is akin to planning a trip back from your destination, then along your proposed route to the point of origin. In effect, you "scope out" the journey before beginning.   Experiment and determine whether this process works for you, too.

A Matter of Choice

Let's return to the Payne Expedition letter on pages 99–100 for a moment before turning attention to a similar message that succeeded. Ask how you'd characterize the original closing: "I'd appreciate your giving it some thought, John, and then getting back in touch with me." Suggestive? (It would have to improve even to be slotted in this category.) Yet this wasn't an **Information only** letter. So the writer made an inappropriate choice, as reflected in the wording. Better to have closed on a *Direct* or *Provocative* note.

In the *Closing,* as in the *Opening* and the *Body,* we're continually concerned with *Tone,* the first of the four structural elements serving as linchpins of discussion in this book. Let's compare the tone of this next message, a memo proposal which succeeded, with that of the communication to John Marshall, which failed:

Successful Message:

> *TO: Data Systems Manager*
> *FROM: Operations Clerks*

We have found a way to get products to users on a timely basis. An increased processing load and interrupted file orders are leading causes for product shipment delay.

<u>Current Situation</u>

Products most often arrive when our people are not scheduled. Data Systems operates only Tuesday through Saturday and either early in the day or later in the evening.

In addition, line organization requirements often filter through several management responsibilities. The result is that priorities are lost or forgotten. Necessary two-way communication and followup are lacking.

<u>Our Proposal</u>

First, establish a two-shift operation in the distribution areas: from 3:00 a.m. to 11:30 a.m., and from 9:00 a.m. to 6:00 p.m. Each shift would run from Tuesday through Saturday.

Second, change supervisory organization to create an area dedicated to serving clerical requirements. Intra-office goals and priorities can be coordinated between the clerical managers and supervisors with the new service-oriented section.

(Some drawbacks are inherent with this proposal, such as increasing the workforce to handle coverage and receiving products after the scheduled shift end. But, the following benefits far outweigh any drawbacks.)

<u>Benefits</u>

1) Coverage when products are most likely to be produced and available.
2) Commitments and product goals between areas.
3) Improved service to and from the printers at a significant monthly cost

> *savings.*
> *4) Computer backlogs resolved without*
> *involving reject re-entry clerks.*
> *5) Position rejects reduced in cycle age.*

Conclusion

> *We are confident this proposal can help us deliver products*
> *when due. May we have your approval by October 23?*

Diagnostic Approach

We'll first take an at-a-glance look at the entire message, which is what readers tend to do subconsciously, anyway. The look is reader-friendly: concise paragraphs, headings and a list used, overall document brief. We're drawn into the message rather than locked out.

What's the sender's objective? To get a proposal approved. The writer's *Tone* is conversational, forthright, businesslike — the argument is laid out convincingly to "sell" the reader. Note that the *Emphatic Opening* presents a solution to a problem rather than the problem itself. In fact, the first draft opened this way: *"Products are not getting to the user on a timely basis."*

When you compare the draft opening with the final version, you can see that the original doesn't coax the reader into the writer's corner. Problem statements are off-putting (and all too easy to generate). Emphasizing the obverse — the good news — takes a little digging, but pays off by stacking the deck in your favor. Don't just problem shuffle in your messages, rather *problem solve*.

Profile & Mechanics

Who is the reader in the sample successful message? Someone up the chain of command from the writer, someone who is familiar with the problem. The reader is a manager, most likely a decision maker with authority to grant proposal approval. I'd say the writer did a good job strategizing before writing, assessing what is significant for the reader to know, detailing benefits, and using familiar language.

The first topic heading, "Current Situation," leads into information providing background, a perspective for the reader on how the situation developed. Originally, the heading was worded "Problem Statement." The revision is neutral, deliberately leaning away from any negative implications. Are you checking sentence length (<20 words) and type (*loose* or *periodic*) in the memo proposal? Notice, too, the use of *active voice*.

Information under the heading "Our Proposal" is two-pronged, conveying action imperatively through verb use. The writer had originally written, "A two-shift operation should be established," and "Changes in supervision should be made," which were passive, declarative, conditional proposal points. Drawbacks, or risks, are discussed, so the writer can't be accused of skipping them. But they're presented in paragraph form and transitioned away from by the statement leading to the "Benefits" topic heading.

Value–Added Document

The benefits certainly do outweigh the drawbacks. They're listed, which draws the eye to them, they're comprehensive, and they're concise. Providing incentive, the benefits cap the info in the *Body* persuasively. Now, the writer can successfully move to the *Closing*, having set up the reader to go along with the action request. (In fact, maybe the heading "Request" would have been more appropriate than "Conclusion." Rather than drawing a conclusion in the *Closing*, the writer is telling where to go from here.)

The first draft of the closing in the example on page 108 read this way: "This proposal should help us deliver products when due. May we have your feedback by October 23?" The "should" is weak and suggestive, detracting from the provocative tone of the final sentence. The version that went out conveys confidence through the *Closing*; the writer is sure of the problem solution. (Guard against conveying arrogance or cockiness when choosing *Direct* statements.) "Approval" in the last sentence is preferable to "feedback" because it's specific. Besides, isn't "feedback" the noise made when microphones come in contact with amplifiers?

Combination Doubles Back Around

I'd characterize the proposal memo closing as a combination of *Direct* and *Provocative*. It comes back around full circle to reinforce delivering products when due (the solution) and invites the reader to make a "yes" decision. Of course, the proof of the pudding lies not in how effectively we can critique this message, but in whether it actually received a favorable response. I'm pleased to report it did, and I believe you can readily see why, especially when you compare it to the failed document (pages 99–100), which conveyed no benefits and simply fell off the end of the page in the closing.

Are there substance changes we might make if we were writing either of these documents? Maybe so. But remember: It's not substance problems so much as *style* concerns which cause messages to misfire. The sender of the successful proposal has developed a model to use for future similar messages, although overly heavy reliance on models or form messages can result in institutional boilerplate failing to move the audience. If you have "canned" messages on a word processing disk you just fire off, or a "canned" speech you deliver at various functions, update the content and style periodically to prevent them from becoming stale — either for you or your audiences.

Chapter 5 Review

Here are the key discussion points distilled:

- ☞ Use the *Closing* as the final point of impact with your audience. They'll tend to remember first what they read or hear last.

- ☞ Repeat <u>significant</u> information by reinforcing or summarizing points you made in the *Opening* or *Body*.

- ☞ Tell what happens next. Readers and listeners are wondering, so satisfy their curiosity by detailing specifically.

☞ Choose *Direct, Suggestive,* or
   Provocative Closings — as appropriate.
   Refer to your objective and audience profile.

☞ Stay on track with *Tone.* Make sure you
   "round out" the message if it's <u>Action</u>, or
   conclude definitively if it's <u>Info Only</u>.
   Always maintain effective use of **Message
   Mechanics** into the *Closing*.

"The immature writer imitates. The mature writer steals."
                                        – T. S. Eliot

Overview

At this point, I've concluded presenting and discussing principles and techniques of effective message sending. All the while, you've been following along intently, practicing putting into effect the approaches you've been learning about. But we're not yet finished.

You may have noted that the application exercises had to do with portions of documents that I've guided you through composing or editing for delivery. Now it's time for another gear shift so you can work on an entire document, and critique your own efforts as you go along. Remember, my intent is to prepare you as your own toughest critic. In this chapter you'll get a chance to see how well you do diagnosing and remedying communication deficiencies. In the process you'll measure what learning you've accomplished and analyze where you may still need to concentrate your efforts.

First, I'd like you to look over the detailed checklist on the next page covering the significant points discussed in the preceding chapters. You'll see ten highlights at the top (a summary) presented in itemized form, each point led off by an action verb. Next, I elaborate to provide more explanation, reviewing for you what's most important to remember about each message–sending element.

As you look over the checklist, note that where I discuss *active* and *passive* voice, and *loose* and *periodic* sentences, I use examples of each element.

Quick Reference Checklist

Highlights

1) Organize the message.
2) Profile your audience.
3) Converse with readers and listeners.
4) Choose the appropriate *Tone.*
5) Prefer the active voice and short, loose sentences.
6) Decide which *Opening* you'll use.
7) Don't sag in the middle (*Body*).
8) Add audience incentive.
9) Choose the appropriate *Closing.*
10) Evaluate your messages on a regular basis.

*   *   *

Organize Message – Do you want to persuade, provoke action, or merely inform? Is the information positive, negative, or neutral? What reaction do you want from the audience?

Profile Audience – Target to their self interests. Ask whether members are superiors, peers, or subordinates. Who are the decision makers? What will motivate them?

Converse – Speak clearly and directly, and try to write the way you speak. Be able to shift between formal/informal, personal/impersonal, objective/subjective modes.

Choose Tone – Tone is attitude, or how you come across. Should you be assertive, demanding, apologetic? Would humor be appropriate? Once you choose a tone, keep it consistent.

Use Active Verbs – Use active verbs for clarity, directness, and conciseness. Passive verbs, on the other hand, are to be used if a change in emphasis is desired. They are also useful if you're choosing a tactful or politically sensitive tone.

Keep Sentences Short – When speaking, our sentences average under 20 words. Check that they do when you write. Keep words concrete. The less abstract the wording, the greater the likelihood the message will be understood and favorably reacted to.

Use Loose Sentences – Use loose sentences (i.e., with the main idea up front) when you want directness. If, on the other hand, ideas are to be suspended for the audience until the end, use periodic sentences (i.e., with the main idea before the period or stop). You've just read a loose, then a periodic sentence.

Choose Your Opening – Which approach is appropriate: *Emphatic* or *Low-key*? An effectively thought-out opening provides a pathway through the rest of the message. It contains a statement of purpose and focuses the audience on content.

Organize the Body – Use *Content Mapping* to corral your thoughts and avoid sag in the middle. Check for audience friendliness, idea flow sequence, and use of headings & lists. Consider visual depictions in written messages, and visual aides when speaking. Tables, charts, graphs, or illustrations tell a visual story.

State Benefits – Clearly state the value or "why" of any action/decision/position that you want the audience to take. Check your message outline for completeness. Ask, "What's in the message for my audience?" This will ensure that you add incentive to persuade or motivate.

Avoid the *Tennis-Match Syndrome* – When using past, present, and future tense, don't jump around from each and back again in the same written paragraph or speech section. Keep thoughts orderly to avoid a jarring mix of elements.

Employ Variety – Use variety in vocabulary choice, sentence length, paragraph length, verb voice, and style, as appropriate. Variety affects readability and hearability.

Use Lists – Lists add message clarity and emphasis. They can appear in the middle of a paragraph, with information itemized by bullets, numbers, letters, and the like. But don't overuse "grocery lists" of data, and be sure to lead in and wrap up when listing.

Close Effectively – The most remembered part of a business communication is what is read or heard last. Make it count. Tie the closing to the opening for an *Action* message; be succinct in stating what you want the audience to do. If the message is *Info only*, restate a significant point. Keep in mind the three closing categories: *Direct, Suggestive, Provocative.*

Pareto Principle

Incidentally, I'm applying the Pareto Principle to the book's concepts at this point. The principle comes to us from Economics, and simply stated it says that:

> *"Significant items in a group normally constitute a small portion of the total items."*

In other words, if you receive a report containing 30 recommendations, you can usually safely assume that not all 30 carry equal weight. A core or nucleus of, say, 5 or 6 of the recommendations will be most significant. The trick is determining which are most important. If **Content Mapping** had been used in the report, the sender would have grouped the recommendations by priority, saving the reader some labor intensity.

Another way of looking at the Pareto Principle is in terms of the widely known "80/20" rule: 80 percent of wealth is controlled by 20 percent of the population; 80 percent of crimes are committed by 20 percent of the population; 80 percent of oil wells are located on 20 percent of the land . . . and so on. Certainly, the percentages don't always break down neatly into 80/20, but you get the idea. Similarly, my checklist doesn't recap every single point made previously in this book, but it boils the *significant* information down for you in at-a-glance fashion.

Taking Measure

You'll find the checklist handy to refer to for quick refresher information. It may be particularly useful with this next exercise, designed to sharpen your diagnostic skills. Even though I'm asking you to critique "someone else's" ability, you'll take the same approach with your own messages. And evaluating your own communication style (and substance) is the most efficient way to measure what you've learned.

The process becomes a test, so to speak, making relevant use of this book's content *as it applies to your own particular message sending needs.* But, of course, even though I use the word "test," I don't mean to induce achievement stress in you the way those schoolteachers from long ago did. The exercise is not intended to intimidate but to elucidate.

Here's a letter to a vendor; read it over and then go through the series of questions that follow:

> *This week I was called into a meeting with my manager and designer. They discussed the design of the container package you now supply us. While it was agreed that the package performs well in a functional capacity, they feel that a new, modernized design would better attract customers and enhance sales.*
>
> *Perhaps you could render a new package by changing something about either the current package look, printing, etc. Costs could be amortized through increased sales. We would appreciate you sending a design change proposal. It is our hope and intention to retain you as a supplier long into the future.*

This exercise may remind you of those deliberately misdrawn illustrations you saw in activity books from childhood — "Spot the 6 things wrong in this picture." Let's see what patterns we can spot in this letter and how we can improve the message:

■<u>Are the writer's thoughts collected</u>? You should be able to readily determine the message objective and desired reader reaction.

■<u>What does the reader profile indicate</u>? What do you determine to be characteristic of the relationship between writer and reader?

■<u>Is the writer conversing on paper</u>? Will the reader understand the meaning of "amortized" in the second paragraph?

■<u>Is the Tone appropriate</u>? How would you characterize the writer's attitude? Does he or she seem to be at a distance from the message? (Note the use of first-person pronouns.)

■Does the writer prefer the <u>active voice</u> and <u>short, loose sentences</u>?

■<u>Is the Opening *Emphatic* or *Low-key*</u>? Isn't the first statement likely to prompt a "so what" reaction?

■<u>Does the message "sag" in the middle</u>? Where's the conciseness, the evidence of **Content Mapping**?

■<u>Does the Body contain reader incentive</u>? Don't get eye strain trying to find missing benefits.

■<u>Is the appropriate Closing used</u>? What happens next? The closing just fizzles.

Notice that the nine questions underlined above correspond to the first nine Highlights from the Quick Reference Checklist (page 114). You can review your messages quickly and efficiently by asking the same questions *before* the message goes out (as part of your editing procedure) and *after* the message is delivered (as a self-check to do better next time).

Personal Review

I strongly recommend setting aside about an hour of "slow time" each month (if there is such a thing!) for critiquing your style and skills to keep both sharp. Investing time for review pays dividends of maintaining consistency and continuing improvement. Take a tip from time management experts: We don't *find* the time for important efforts; we *make* it. And evaluating over time is critically important.

If you don't use what you've learned in this book — or in any other course of study, for that matter — you tend to lose it. Referring to the Pareto Principle again, educational studies show that in a very short time after learning material of nearly any kind, we tend to forget up to 80% of the material . . . *unless* we repeatedly put into practice what we've learned. So the best way to minimize the forgetfulness factor is to get into the habit of evaluating your efforts at least monthly so you can monitor your behavior objectively.

The day we deliver a talk or write a message we're a little too close to the forest to see the trees. A subjective emotional attachment forms to the communication we're generating. After a few weeks go by, though, we can better appraise the message in the cold light of day, and spot significant aspects of it — both positive and negative — enabling us to build on previous efforts.

Critical Period of Impact

Keep in mind that your messages, whatever their nature, tend to have very short lifespans. Decisions are made on your communications typically within the first 24 to 72 hours after they are delivered. Then they quickly become as stale as yesterday's newspaper. In fact, according to the Dartnell Corporation for business research in Chicago, the odds are fewer than 1 in 20 that you or anyone else will ever look at an originally written message *at any time again* once it's read after it's been generated. Our spoken communications are even more fleeting. Unless they're recorded — or composed and delivered with impact — they go unremembered. And, too often, that means they go unresponded to.

Of course, exceptions do occur. For example, many recommendation reports survive long enough to serve as discussion matter at subsequent meetings. So they often live longer than 72 hours. And other written or spoken messages may be reread or recalled at much later dates. But if they are, it's because they somehow *register significantly* for the audience. I don't want my messages to come back and haunt me; rather, I want to be able to point to them with pride because of how exceptionally well planned and executed they are. The English Romantic writer William Blake said that execution is the chariot of genius. Let's, then, become proficient at the *process* which enables us to generate a well-received *product*, namely, our business and personal communications.

> [**Obiter dicta:** The comedian Don Novello (Father Guido
>   Sarducci on *Saturday Night Live*) once cited statistics
>   claiming that college graduates forget up to 95%
>   of four years of study within only a number of
>   months after receiving their diplomas. His solution:
>   Start teaching only the 5% people remember — a
>   great way to cut down on time and money spent
>   chasing baccalaureate degrees!]

Supplier Letter Revision

Let's take a look at a rewrite to the letter from page 117, checking for *ownership, enthusiasm,* and *incentive*:

> *Would you be interested if we could give you a*
> *considerable order increase for container*
> *packages?*
>
> *Our sales manager, designer, and I met this*
> *week to discuss the design of the container*
> *package you regularly supply. We believe that*
> *incorporating graphics with printing will*
> *better attract customers and enhance sales.*
> *So, I'm enclosing our designer's mockup for*
> *you to look over. No doubt you'll have*
> *suggestions for making it even better.*
>
> *Our intent is to keep your retooling costs to a*
> *minimum, and we're confident that increased*
> *orders to you — from us and our contractors—*

*will justify the expense. We're hoping to keep
you as a supplier long into the future if we can
get a container package design that meets our
objectives.*

*Will you call me by July 1st and let me know
how we can get started on the graphics?*

Comparing the two versions of the letter reveals the nuts and bolts of what the essential message is, and how best to convey it. A reminder, though: there's no one right way of writing or saying anything. What I'm trying to get at is the most effective, productive way each time out — given your *objective* and *audience profile* considerations.

Finished Product

You'll recall that one of the examples I used in Chapter 1, when discussing outlining techniques, was a hypothetical message to a boss regarding the IBM Personal System 2 computer. In Chapter 4, we looked at a suggested paragraph which might appear in the body of such a message. [The examples I used then had to do with *loose* and *periodic* paragraphs. See Chapter 4, page 86.]

What might the memo look like in its entirety? Here's a suggested version:

*We need to decide whether the IBM Personal System 2 will
best serve our department's growing needs.*

*Each month, we can achieve a savings of about
$12,000 and a productivity boost of 5%, according to a
recent Stacon Consulting study. The P/S 2 can help us
get these results by automating reference tasks and
freeing staffers to concentrate on marketing duties.*

*P/S 2 software is usable with our department's
PC's, so converting won't be a problem. Neither
will training, because the P/S 2 complements the system
our staff is now familiar with. The P/S 2 allows us to*

> *upgrade with minimal workflow disruption, providing increased capability as we meet anticipated growth. Each model unit (hardware and software) currently retails in the $2200–$7500 range.*
>
> *I suggest we attend the local IBM exhibit next week so we can see a P/S 2 demonstration and judge for ourselves. Are you available Tuesday morning?*

As we've been doing, critiquing the document by applying the first 9 highlights from the checklist on page 114 shows how effectively written it is. The memo serves as a good example of how to establish the appropriate *Tone* when writing up the chain of command. Note that the Closing doesn't ask for approval to purchase; it co-opts the reader into the decision-making process. Pay particular attention in your own message sending to whether you're making up your audience's minds for them, or leading them to the brink of a decision but letting them make the leap for themselves.

Writing Tripod

This geometric figure is another of my attempts to graphically encapsulate some of the verbal message in this book. (And, in the process, appeal to those of you who are left–brain readers! Or is it right–brain??)

Easily Toppled

We all know that a tripod is a three–legged object requiring a balanced weight distribution to keep it from toppling over. Atop the tripod is "Results." That's what we're trying to achieve — to sustain — when we communicate. Each of the three legs plays a crucial role in the tripod's design . . . as well as, analogously, in helping us accomplish message–sending objectives:

First, *practice* putting into application the principles and techniques presented in this book. I've mentioned this important concept before, and I'm reiterating it now. Keep in mind, as they tried to teach us in school, that it's not just practice that makes perfect, but the *right kind* of practice. Just what do you practice, especially if your back is to the wall and you haven't got time to search through the book and all its examples? Here's a quick and effective approach, one I've recently mentioned: Use highlights 1–9 at the top of the checklist on page 114.

Second, *edit* your message before delivery. To edit means to prepare for publication or presentation. If you've picked up on the written and oral communication skills I've presented, then you've been learning how to edit along the way. Shape the message so it best presents both you and what you want to convey to your audience. Check to make sure you're adhering to proper spelling, diction, grammar, and punctuation. Here's where it's often helpful to bounce the message off a friend or co-worker, seeking constructive criticism. Polish the document or rehearse the speech with allies who can act as sounding boards and help you fine tune the "best-foot-forward" version.

Third, *evaluate* your message after the fact. This important debriefing stage corresponds to highlight 10 from the *Quick Reference Checklist* — evaluate your messages regularly. It's common good-sense business practice to periodically assess activity and make sure it's getting results. Communications, though, are often overlooked when it comes time to reassess, with the unwanted result that bad habits are propagated, and the same old mistakes are made over and over again.

Make sure you give equal effort to each leg of the tripod. You'll then be doing what's necessary to ensure that you achieve the aims you had in mind for communicating in the first place.

Costs

Workshop participants frequently ask me how much business communications cost. I typically answer that determining costs isn't easy; at best we can only estimate. And it isn't just monetary costs I think we should be keeping in mind. What about human costs? In 1978, I saw the results of a Government Accounting Office survey which estimated the cost per page of a written business communication at $12.50. This figure was arrived at as the result of a complicated equation which factored in:

- the average annual U.S. white–collar salary at the time (about $16,000, as I recall)

- the amount of time necessary to research, compose and edit a document (which worked out to something like an hour per page)

- secretarial, storage, retrieval, duplication and postage costs

Ten years later, that figure was computed by a number of other surveys to have risen to $40 per page, an increase of nearly 400%. I can believe it. Hasn't *everything* gone up about that much since 1978? (Except wages.) In fact, these days, some surveys put the cost 200% higher — at about $80 per page! And remember, that figure represents only a national statistical average.

For example, I know of some organizations spending many times that amount per page to generate oral and written communications. Admittedly, some of the expense is due to waste and mismanagement. But, in businesses where the final product is a service — such as a governmental body — the likelihood of high communication expense can be greater than in businesses where the final product is goods or commodities, such as a manufacturing concern.

Costly End Product

Why so?   Because a large proportion of manhours goes into researching and writing at service organizations. For example, a typical state auditor's office anywhere in the U.S. is in the business of generating only reports as a final product, reports documenting how taxpayers' dollars are spent. All the effort in a 40-hour week goes, ultimately, toward preparing messages.   A car company, however, builds cars. There, a lower percentage of overall effort is channeled into job communications, even though the volume of messages generated may be higher than at a state auditor's office.

Some high-priced law firms might charge as much as $1,500 to write a 2-page will. Can a document really cost that much? Of course not.   You're paying "overhead" for the attorneys' expertise, the firm's prestige, its square-footage lease, and so on. If cost is the only consideration, you'd be better off asking a lawyer you've known for some time (or a recent law-school grad) to draw up a will for you. The expense will amount to hundreds of dollars less, and the document will be just as valid in a court of law as a $1,500 will.

Who Pays?

If you write a ten-page report at work, the expense is about $800 (based on an average cost of about $80 per page). Of course, the money doesn't come out of your pocket, but you can see how it's an ancillary — and often hidden — cost of doing business. I always tell my workshop participants that it doesn't *cost* to communicate effectively so much as it *pays*.

And whatever the expense in terms of dollars spent, the best way to justify cost is to send messages that achieve intended objectives. I wouldn't assert that we can necessarily lower the cost of the communications we generate (although some savings are probably possible). But I would take the position that we can *control* costs by improving skills.

But suppose you write a message that creates ill will? Or give a talk that causes confusion or misunderstanding? It's difficult in these cases to measure the expense not only in terms of dollars but also in terms of *human costs*. And believe me, human costs are very real, and often very expensive. Credibility, reputation, goodwill can be on the line — all, in the final analysis, very real costs. So even though I can't quantify them, I want to remain sensitive to the fact that human costs can have more impact on business success than dollar costs.

Before and After

Time again to analyze a communication in first-draft form, then its revision after the techniques described in this book have been applied:

> *There are a number of us who do not want to put offloading cranes on the cargo ships unless we absolutely have to; and there are a number of us who consider the need for cranes obvious. Without question cranes are costly to install, costly to maintain, have adverse effects on work-team size, and reduce the overall container lift capacity. On the other hand, the arguments in favor of cranes may be summarized as follows:*

> *Approximately 20% of the projected revenues come from ports that have no cranes. And a shipboard crane will supplement port cranes when traffic is heavy and hence reduce the lost time in port. Floating cranes may work, but not with the efficiency of a shipboard crane.*

> *Our conclusion is that we have given realistic estimates for installing and maintaining the cranes, and that either of the two reasons above appears economically to justify installing the cranes. If they help generate revenue in a tough, competitive situation or reduce port time, the costs of installation and maintenance are more than offset.*

Put on your thinking cap and take a few minutes to rewrite the letter on a separate sheet of paper. There's no time limit, so take your time. But *do complete* the exercise to make the most of what I've been putting across throughout the book.

Here's my revision:

> *We recommend installing offloading cranes on ships for the following reasons:*
>
> > *1) 80% of revenues come from ports with cranes. We can penetrate that market.*
> > *2) Shipboard cranes supplement port cranes when traffic is heavy and reduce lost port time.*
> > *3) Shipboard cranes are more efficient than floating cranes.*
>
> *Costs to install and maintain are easily offset by the volume of cargo and revenue which offloading cranes allow. Granted, work team size and overall container lift capacity are affected, but not enough to recommend against installing.*
>
> *If we can get your approval right away, we can start installing cranes before the heavy ship-ping season begins June 1.*

I've been guiding you in your analyses up until now. But at this point I'm going to cut you loose to make your own comparisons and, more important, draw your own conclusions. Don't be disappointed if your revision doesn't closely resemble mine. Remember, there's no "be–all & end–all." You only set yourself up for failure if you try to achieve according to how someone else would perform.

Rather, try for achieving according to the best you yourself are capable of. Set your own standards. Find your own comfort zone where style is concerned. (Do you recall what I wrote earlier in this book? Style is always a reflection of *individual* personality.) On the other hand, if your revision does match mine closely, congratulations!

You're obviously clever, intelligent, and already successful at message sending.

Your Bread–and–Butter Communications

The acid test of how well you're able to apply the approaches this book details has little, in the long run, to do with how effectively you revise someone else's messages. It has to do with how effective you are from here on out with your own on–the–job and personal communications. If you've been following along, paying attention, *thinking*, and trying, then you've been learning — which boils down to becoming better equipped to handle situations that are "for keeps."

Your bread–and–butter letters, memos, reports, E–mail, speeches, briefings, proposals, and presentations will constitute the proving grounds for how successfully the lessons in this book take. I can assure you you'll do well over time with practice and persistence. You may not notice overnight changes in your effectiveness at message sending. But within weeks you'll start to realize positive reactions from your audiences, a boost of confidence in your attitude, and a feeling of having greater control over the outcome of your interactive communications. "There's nothing to it but to do it" and, in the doing, improve oneself.

In Conclusion: An Object Lesson

We can all learn one of life's lasting lessons from the experience of E.F. Schumacher, 20th Century economist and humanist, who underwent a significant conversion of thought in mid–life. Schumacher's conversion was brought about in large measure by reading William Prescott's book, *Conquest of Mexico*, first published in 1909. In a passage of particularly penetrating insight for Schumacher, Prescott observed that modern man's paralysis is similar to that of the Aztecs when they met Cortez and his men sitting on horses, equipped with firearms. It was not so much the power of the Spaniards that destroyed the Aztec empire as it was *the disbelief of the Aztecs in themselves*.

When you think about it, isn't the starting point for success quite simply attitude? Believe in yourself, then act on that belief, and you create a means of achieving.

Success in any endeavor comes about largely through a combination of positive mental outlook and sheer dint of effort. The 100th blow of a sledgehammer may be the one that breaks through a brick wall. But it takes 99 blows beforehand for that one to have its effect.

To communicate successfully isn't easy. It comes with a price tag. You'll decide whether the price is worth paying by staying with it or giving up. The way to get good at something isn't to save yourself for only those occasions requiring your best effort. What is it you're "storing up," anyway? Non-activity?

Stick–to–it–iveness

The way toward becoming proficient — being the best — is to *spend* yourself: to put forth active effort, repeatedly, until you get good at whatever it is you're doing. Stay with it long enough, and you'll improve in spite of yourself. I wish they'd taught us these lessons of life in school. But maybe some of them simply aren't transmittable. It seems every generation has to mine all over again for itself those valuable nuggets of information. Maybe, at best, the only thing previous generations can do is hand over the pick and show us where to start swinging.

And maybe that's as it should be. How many times have we all heard that we appreciate something more when it's hard–earned? (Okay, I'm not sure *I* totally buy that, either.) But I do subscribe — heartily — to the belief that some things which are handed to us do diminish in value. Next time you sit down to write a letter or compose a speech, remember these words of Gene Fowler, noted American journalist: "*Writing is easy; all you do is sit with a blank sheet of paper in front of you until drops of blood form on your forehead.*" He could have mentioned the sweat and tears, too.

Aim High

This stirring passage from the writings of Teddy Roosevelt conveys the state of mind I'm advocating when you embark on worthy tasks:

> *"Far better it is to dare mighty things, to win*
> *glorious triumphs, even though checkered by*
> *failure, than to take rank with those poor spirits*
> *who neither enjoy much nor suffer much,*
> *because they live in the gray twilight that knows*
> *neither victory nor defeat."*

Okay, it's your turn. Start with wanting to do better, and then actually *do* something about it. In fact, you're already on that track. After all, you've read this book. You're more than halfway there.

It's all downhill from this point.

*   *   *   *

The information that follows comprises an **Appendix** with specific oral-presentation reference data, four supplemental **Articles**, **Resources** for pursuing improvements further, and an **Editing/Proofreading Manual** for helping you make more informed language choices in any communications context.

Specific Tips For Public Speaking

Below are some signs that mark poor speakers. Most are simply subconscious nervous mannerisms. To change them, you first have to be aware of them. When you have the opportunity, videotape yourself making a presentation, and check for these signs during playback. It's also helpful to watch for each in evidence the next time you take in a talk:

√ <u>Bobbing on your feet</u>. Resist the temptation to rise up on the balls of your feet and lower back down on your heels. Plant yourself and hold your ground.

√ <u>Using fillers</u>. This is perhaps the most frequently inhabited refuge of speakers, even seasoned presenters who are quite comfortable in the spotlight. We've all heard the barrage of "uh," "um," "er," "ah," and the like tumbling from the lips of speakers who aren't fully prepared or are inordinately nervous. Some filler use is natural and even okay. *Some*. But to smooth out your vocal style, rehearse or prepare in depth, and *listen* to yourself (or tape record) as you talk.

√ <u>Talking too fast</u>. Yes, the solution is to slow down. But "achievement stress" may be operating. If your delivery is rapid-fire, actively practice pacing yourself. Go over your text beforehand. Have a friendly critiquer listen to make sure you're enunciating clearly. For example, don't gloss over letters like the "t" in "interview" so it sounds like "innerview," or the final "g" in "ing" words (like "goin'" for "going"). Pronounce carefully and completely all syllables of each word. Take heart in the fact that studies do show that speaking somewhat quickly can be a plus, energizing listeners to pay attention and keep up with you. But don't pull a "John Marchetta." (You may remember

him as the fast-talking actor who did the Federal
Express commercials a few years ago.)

√   Droning. This is just the opposite of talking
too fast.   We've all heard droners at after-
dinner speeches or in classroom lectures.
Monotonic delivery bores listeners, dampening
presentation of subject matter that could
otherwise be enlivening. The solution is to
maintain a conversational cadence.

√   Failing to vary, pause, or gesture. Don't try
merely to "get through" the talk.   You'll lose
the audience, and you may tend to rush, glossing
over important topics. Practice voice inflection.
Listen to your rehearsal tapes for how you can
better modulate and resonate your pitch. Don't
be shy about using your eyes, face, hands, arms
to punctuate points you're making.   No one likes
to sit before a wooden-Indian style of presenter.

Psychological Appeal

A tried-and-true method of infusing your oral presentations with
energy and dynamism is to tie your message, as appropriate, to
common human desires. For example, here are 16 objects of desire (in
no particular order) which psychologists identify as common to all
human beings:

1. Security	9. Appreciation
2. Popularity	10. Enjoyment (pleasure)
3. Health	11. Sexual attraction
4. Pain avoidance	12. Money
5. Praise	13. Appetite satisfaction
6. Style	14. Opportunity
7. Creativity	15. Success
8. Self-confidence	16. Leisure time

It's not too farfetched to look for ways of integrating one or more
of these desires into your talk, to make sure you strike an interest
chord for your audience. Do you see ways of developing a theme for

your speech incorporating any of these desired elements? For example, *Money* and *Success* are naturals to weave into a talk on investment strategies; *Health* and *Appetite Satisfaction* into a presentation on diet control.

Writing The Speech

In addition to using the techniques in this book designed to help prepare written documents, I have some specific advice for writing your speech or talk, then condensing it so you don't have to memorize word-for-word:

☞ Use lots of paper with plenty of space between lines.
   If you're using a typewriter or word processor, triple space.
☞ Next, go back over your message and jot down the main
   ideas (take a cue from your outline) on index cards.
☞ Check for the flow of ideas:

Introduction – *Emphatic*

Open with the issue that's most significant for your audience. Work on getting their attention with an impactful beginning. At the start, they want you to give them something they can latch on to. Don't disappoint them.

Body – *Organized*

Emphasize the main points relating to your topic. Itemize — in 1,2,3 or A,B,C fashion. Here's where your outline and **Content Mapping** come in. Remember that listeners' attention spans ebb and flow in 20-minute cycles. Pay attention to pacing and the rhythm of your idea flow.

Conclusion – *Direct, Suggestive,* or *Provocative*

Recap your key points and let the audience know what, if anything, happens next. Keep your ideas concise and your summary brief. Remember: People retain longest what they hear last. Use the conclusion as a final point of impact with your listeners.

☞ Consider <u>Tone</u>, which is your attitude as a speaker. Be enthusiastic. Get behind your subject matter. Tone is critical in conveying favorable impressions.

☞ As you draft your talk, stop and read aloud various sections. How do they sound? Do they instinctively ring true? Are you being conversational?

☞ Do more than one version of the text. Rewriting fine tunes your presentation. Preparing will be time well spent.

Come Across

Successful speakers are able to project: their voice, their attitude, their believability, themselves; they establish and demonstrate a *presence*. Speak to everyone before you so you can be heard by all. Plan to come across effectively to each individual audience member, no matter how many people are there to listen to you.

And remember to *sell*. Take a tip from marketing techniques. Advertisers remind us that the best ads aren't the ones which prompt us to say, "Isn't that clever!" but those which make us take out the pocketbook and buy. That means being able to persuade.

Linchpins of Persuasion/Effective Selling

Benefits play an important role in speechmaking, just as they do in action-oriented written communications. In any type of message sending, it's crucial to present facts, and to let those facts speak for themselves as convincing, persuading presentation points. Especially in talks, give examples where possible. For instance, if a salesman were delivering a briefing on quarterly activity and trying to boost efforts, he could say:

> "*Sales last quarter were 6 percent below projections. Now, we can point to economic conditions, to shipment delays, to increased competition. But we can't deny that we just didn't try hard enough. For instance, I had opportunities for callbacks that I just let slide. Every callback is a potential customer. So, to get all of us to do a better job next quarter, the manager who gets his sales the highest above*

projections will win a trip to Hawaii."

Note the incentive — the benefit — to prod desired behavior.

Advice You Can Use

No matter what type of talk you deliver, keep this advice in mind:

■ <u>Speak from the heart.</u> Be honest about your emotions. Mean what you say. Audiences *want* you to get behind your message. Build your presentation on a foundation of integrity.

■ <u>Believe in your material.</u> Demonstrate confidence. Don't try to tack sincerity on; make sure it derives organically from your motivation for speaking in the first place.

■ <u>Build interest.</u> Don't keep listeners in suspense. Tell them right away what's important, then why, then give supporting information. How does your message affect them? (Remember that people tend to behave in terms of what satisfies their self-interests.)

■ <u>Move your audience.</u> Appeal to their emotions. Try to make them different people from who they were before you began talking. This is a tall order, I know, but ask yourself what they're going to gain from hearing you that they wouldn't get otherwise. How can you educate them?

■ <u>Let your personality come through.</u> Your uniqueness as a presenter is as much a part of your delivery as what you have to say. Let the best of your self surface. What are you most certain about? Where does your competence lie? Here's your opportunity to show what you know, to exhibit your particular talent. Maybe

you're a good joke teller, or are able to convey
sympathy effectively. Put these traits to use.

Give thought to your overall style. Don't fall into the category of
speaker demonstrated in the following anecdote:

*A man took the podium in a large meeting room at a convention and
began droning on. Not long after he began, the first of the
audience members began to exit. Within 15 minutes the audience
had dwindled to one person. The speaker kept going, finally
concluding his talk 10 minutes later. The last person left in the
audience applauded. When the presenter came down and thanked
the man for staying and then asked him why he had done so, the
answer was, "Because I'm the next speaker."*

How to Polish Your Presentation

Putting the finishing touches on your style is a simple matter of
knowing which ingredients are part of the mix. Here are ways to go
about making your speech a function of thorough preparation:

• Take in other people's speeches. Critique their style. Focus
on aspects of their behavior you'd like to emulate. Pay particular
attention to network newscasters and heads of organizations.
These are usually "smooth delivery" people. Many politicians of
national standing are excellent speakers. It's helpful, also, to
join a Toastmasters group in your community or a speaker's
bureau where you work. These organizations give you a forum to
practice, invaluable in honing public–speaking skills.

• Humanize your message. Push the people–response button
among your listeners by giving real–life illustrations in your talk.
Tell stories, relate anecdotes. These methods drive home the
relevance of what you're saying, help to lend support, clarity and
credibility to your topics, and personalize your subject matter.

• Use natural gestures to punctuate points you make. Your
speech doesn't necessarily have to be stirring or rousing. But a
little body animation on your part can underscore parts of your
message. Use your head, face, arms, and hands to accent key

information elements. Guard against artificiality. Wild gestures are inappropriate. Most of us tend to be naturally expressive with our eyes and hands when we speak. Think about how you come across and be aware of body mannerisms that you can use to your advantage.

* Go with your material. This quality gives your talk life in all its facets. If the situation is emotional, get emotional. It's okay to be humorous at a *roast*, to be somber during a *eulogy*. Doing so allows your audience to "feel" with you, adding an extra dimension of appeal.

Examples to Emulate

Many, many great speakers come to mind when I think of suggesting people whose style and manner are well worth emulating. I'll mention two: Martin Luther King, Jr., and Mario Cuomo. We've all seen and heard clips of King speaking, especially his "I have a dream" speech in August 1963 in Washington. The palpable emotion in his voice, the very real hope in his heart, radiated from the man in waves.

I know it was a very impressionable speech for me and for millions of others. It typifies the very essence, the very stuff of efficient speechmaking: powerful, persuasive, memorable; in short, *effective*.

Mario Cuomo delivered the keynote address at the 1984 Democratic convention. He layered his presentation with facts, with statistics, with heartfelt appeal for a more caring America. I remember as I listened being moved, feeling Cuomo reaching out through words and touching a chord deep within me.

Think of others like these examples: Winston Churchill, Ann Richards (Texas Governor), John F. Kennedy, Hillary Rodham Clinton, for instance. Am I saying you have to be as good as they are to be successful? No. I am saying that by their examples they present us with an opportunity to pick up on what works and to try the same approaches ourselves.

[**Obiter dicta:** Whatever you do, *don't* emulate the example of William Henry Harrison, our 9th

President. His inaugural speech lasted several
hours in blustery March weather, 1841. He developed
pneumonia and died a month later. Longwindedness
can be hazardous to your health.]

Delivery Methods

When you're actually up there in front of your audience, here are
steps to practice to keep your delivery on track:

◙ Concentrate on the task at hand. Maintain contact
with your audience. Paying attention is a two-way
street. You want your audience to give you consideration. Give them consideration, too. Come
prepared. Make it evident that you cared enough
to prepare and practice, to make this experience
worth their while.

I'll admit that, sometimes, there's no substitute for
years of experience. I've given scores of presentations in the past 17 years, and I've gotten measur-
ably better at each one. I shudder to think how I
used to come across in those early years. But, at
some point, each of us has to take the podium and
begin. When you concentrate, when you focus on
your audience, they'll reciprocate. (You might
even find that self-conscious thoughts are dis-
pelled while you "live outside yourself " for the
duration of your speech.)

◙ Have legibly prepared outline or index cards in front
of you. This practice helps in giving structure
to your talk and in picking out key phrases you
want to emphasize. The preferred — and easiest —
talk to give is one you've presented many times
before. But you don't want your talk to have a
"canned" quality. Referring to cards or prepared
pages (or holding an open book or binder in hand)
isn't necessarily distracting to your audience.
Lack of speaker preparation is. Rehearse
using the cue cards, especially if your speech

will be lengthy.

This begs the question, "How long should my talk be?" Well, certainly long enough to get your main points across. But remember the human 20-minute attention span. If you're conducting a 2-day training workshop, take frequent stretch breaks and make the participants' involvement interactive. Use handouts to elaborate important points. Use flipcharts or overhead transparencies to demonstrate what you're discussing.

▣ On your index cards or notes, highlight "trig-ger phrases" that will jostle your memory. For instance, for a talk on finances a friend gave, he typed in caps this phrase on an index card:

"X-RATE TIED TO M.P."

No, there was nothing lewd or prurient about the note to himself. This trigger phrase re-minded him to explain that, "The exchange rate is tied to monetary policy." And he was pre-pared to elaborate for his audience a detailed discussion on this topic.

▣ Memorize what you can. But keep your presentation fluid. And have notes handy in case you "black out." (Ever lose your place while reciting a prayer, for example, and have to start all over again at the beginning?) For most of my presentations I use flipcharts with prepared pages. So I know what's on them. They serve, in effect, as my cue cards should I ever digress or lose my train of thought.

Memorizing works best for very brief presenta-tions. Guard against an overly rigid reliance on your powers of recall. Unless you know the material cold, they may fail you.

▣ Pay attention to appearance. For an important

presentation, your personal grooming is important
to create a favorable impression. Before you even
begin speaking, your audience is judging you on
the basis of how you look. This may not be fair,
but it's a reality. Present yourself in the best possible
light.

Not long ago, I coached a group of aerospace
engineers for a presentation to Air Force officers.
I admonished them to wear their best suits and to
keep their jackets buttoned at all times. Few
things so detract from a talk as the sight of a pro-
truding paunch when an arm is extended holding
a pointer.

Ideal Method

Unfortunately, there is no "ideal method" for learning either how
best to prepare a presentation or how to deliver it. The way this
particular aspect of interpersonal interaction works is demonstrated
in the following advice from the Nobel Prize–winning Irish playwright,
Bernard Shaw, who for much of his life cultivated public speaking
skills. Shaw once related that:

> "*I learned to address an audience as a man learns
> to skate or to cycle— by doggedly making a fool
> of myself until I got used to it.*"

Getting used to it is the trick. Being dogged is a real good start
toward that end.

Prepare, Prepare, Prepare

You can learn to speak extemporaneously, which, by the way, does
not mean "winging it." While some of us are better than others at
thinking on our feet, most of us need some kind of preparation. In
fact, the second definition of the word "extemporaneous" from the
American Heritage Dictionary is, "Prepared in advance, but delivered
without notes or text."

The key element here is *prepared in advance.* You know what you want to say, but you leave the exact method of presentation open. With that said, I now offer a distillation of the steps discussed in this section for at-a-glance reference the next time you have the opportunity to make a speech. It comes as close to an "ideal method" as I can suggest:

* Type out on index cards key brief concept phrases to remind you of points to develop. Establish an idea sequence and number the cards.

* Go over the material. Research it. Fill in the gaps. *Learn it.* Rehearse your delivery with any visual aides you'll use. This is not memorizing as such, but focusing on presentation patterns to add flow to your style.

* Practice before friends, family members, co-workers— anyone you can rope in. Do it over and over again until the presentation takes care of itself. This will help dispel the "fear factor."

* Think of the task as an actor would learning lines for a role. Shakespeare told us that "All the world's a stage, and all the men and women merely players . . . ." You're up in front of your audience to act, and to act convincingly. Successful actors don't merely play a part; they *become* the part.

With An Audience Before You

Here's how it might go during an actual presentation:

■ You stand before your audience, looking straight out at them, and take a deep breath. Then you glance down at your first card: "Intro — diapering baby story." You tell a funny story about diapering a

baby which relates to the subject matter of your
talk.

■ Nervousness recedes as you notice the audience
warming to you. Succeeding phrases on your
cards plug in the memory circuits to your
rehearsals and you transition smoothly into the
Body of your speech.

■ As you continue, your presentation proceeds
naturally. You're making eye contact, speaking
distinctly and enunciating properly, enjoying the
experience. Nothing about your style is canned
as you turn to a chart which details relevant
statistics. You talk from the points on the chart.
You can't lose your place because items are
sequenced.

■ As you near your Conclusion, a buoyant feeling
comes over you. Your manner is flexible,
spontaneous, dynamic — because you're not
locked in to rote line–by–line delivery. Pauses
(which can be powerful devices) allow points
to sink in and to underscore what you have to
say.

■ Your final card indicates "<u>Summary</u>": At this point,
you recap as you wind down, and you may even
ask, once you've finished, whether the audience
has questions. Your final statement is to thank
the audience, with a smile on your face, and then
exit the podium.

Sounds simple, doesn't it? Actually, the situation can present
itself that simply. The method I've just walked you through is an
example of creative visualization. This technique is used by athletes
and others in all walks of life to mentally imagine successfully
completing individual phases of tasks or processes. Think it through
— visualize yourself succeeding — and you sow the seeds for a
positive self–fulfilling prophecy to come about.

The Power To Persuade

Words can move us. Impact and eloquence are very directly functions of the emotional content we invest in language. Read the excerpt below from Shakespeare's play, "The Merchant of Venice." You won't need explanatory context; the passage speaks for itself. Even one-dimensionally, as printed words on a page, the soliloquy (Shylock's speech) has a power to touch us on a deeply human level:

> "*I am a Jew. Hath not a Jew eyes? hath not a Jew*
> *hands,organs, dimensions, senses, affections,*
> *passions? fed with the same food, hurt with the*
> *same weapons, subject to the same diseases,*
> *healed by the same means, warmed and cooled*
> *by the same winter and summer, as a Christian*
> *is? If you prick us, do we not bleed? if you tickle*
> *us, do we not laugh? if you poison us, do we not*
> *die? and if you wrong us, shall we not revenge?*"

Now, imagine those same words spoken by a trained Shakespearean actor, whose elocutionary skills scale the heights of virtuosity. The spoken version adds a dimension which rounds out Shakespeare's intent, the emotional chord he was trying to strike. Very often, spoken messages breathe life into information, making it function differently — and perhaps better — for the receiver.

Sight Or Sound?

Try this experiment the next time you watch TV. Turn down the sound. Watch the picture for a few moments. Now turn the sound up and look away. Which do you miss more, the sight or the sound? That should tell you how important the oral message is.

Man has been writing for only the last 5,500 years or so. Long before alphabet symbols came into existence, mankind had the *sounds* of words. An oral tradition evolves in societies before printed text comes into existence. Stories and shared experiences are passed along from one generation to the next. Every time you make an oral presentation, you're a link in that continuing tradition. So don't shrink from the responsibility, nor take it lightly.

Use the opportunity to further your own ends as well as those of your audience. Rehearse, rely on your ability, and relate what you know. Those are the three R's of successful speechmaking. Mastering them is simple. As I told you earlier, all you have to do is deeply want to succeed, and then work very hard at it.

*   *   *   *   *   *

The following articles provide guideline information related to improved oral presentation techniques. You'll find each useful in targeting specific needs you may have. The pieces that follow are:

√ "Fear of Speaking," by (ahem) Tom Stapleton and Dennis Connor (courtesy Ladies Home Journal)

√ "Speaking with Authority" (courtesy Los Angeles Times)

√ "The Meeting Environment" (courtesy Minnesota Western)

√ "Quick Reference Checklist" — from materials which are part of the Stapleton Communications' *Write It, Speak It!* oral presentations workshop

| *Stapleton Communications* | **FEAR OF SPEAKING**
by Tom Stapleton and Dennis Connor |

What do people fear most in life? Death, loneliness, sickness, flying? Surprisingly enough, none of the above. While these fears rank high, surveys show that far above them ranks speaking before a group.

Few experiences are more intimidating than public speaking. But successful men and women have learned to meet this fear head-on and overcome it. They've had to. Let's face it: your manner of presentation determines how your message is received. No matter who your audience or what your topic, you are attempting to sell yourself and your ideas through public speaking. If called upon to address an audience, would you speak with style or be struck dumb by the spotlight? If you're in the latter group, here are nine symptoms of chronic fear of public speaking and the prescriptions for long-lasting relief:

◆ **Wing-it-itis**. Results in jitters, stammers, and uncertainty. *Remedy*: Solid preparation. First, limit your topic. If you're not thoroughly familiar with the ground you'll cover, research it. Make an outline. Give your speech a beginning, middle, and end. In short, organize.

Next, practice. Set a time limit and pace yourself. Deliver your speech aloud to a tape recorder or friends. When you deliver your talk, your tendency may be to rush, so hold to your practiced, relaxed pace and your presentation will have a better chance of succeeding.

[Should you be called upon to speak without much notice, here are some tips to help you: First, stay calm. Take a few deep breaths and gather your thoughts. Keep your remarks to a minimum and your tone conversational. As soon as possible, ask questions and get your audience involved.]

◆ **Panic/Paralysis**. Terror-induced freeze manifested minutes before delivering a speech. It results in clammy palms, excessive nervous perspiration, and an overwhelming desire to leave town. *Remedy*: Let your nervous system work for you, not against you. There's nothing wrong with being nervous. Your body is preparing for a competitive situation. If you say to yourself, "I appreciate this opportunity; it's my chance to show what I can do," your nervous system will be on your side.

◆ **Shoelace Syndrome**. Morbid fascination with the feet. The sufferer stands hunchbacked, coughs nervously, and stares blankly in the general direction of his or her shoes. *Remedy*: Stand up straight and remember that poor body language can only have a negative effect.

Project a positive image. Assume that everyone is thrilled to be there. Feel free to make gestures that accent what you're saying, and when you speak, let your eyes move around the room, focusing briefly on various people. And try to be aware of unconscious mannerisms that may undermine your delivery, such as scratching yourself or toying with papers.

146

- ◆ **Acute Dullness.** The afflicted becomes listless and exhibits somnambulism. The problem with dullness is that it's contagious. Fortunately, its antidote, enthusiasm, is also infectious. *Remedy*: Open with an attention-getter — a humorous quotation, anecdote, or analogy. Keep your comments vivid and engage your listeners' imagination. This way you'll encourage greater audience participation.

- ◆ **The Drones.** An affliction manifesting itself in monotones or a constant vocal pitch. Listening to a speaker with the drones is like listening to a faucet drip; it grates on your nerves. (Here's where taping yourself comes in handy.) *Remedy*: Go with your material. If it's somber, be somber. If it's exciting, get excited. And if it's humorous, laugh a little.

  Eliminate nervous fillers like "uh" and "you know." Try to maintain a conversational flow. Observe the network newscasters and copy their technique of sight-reading — look at a few sentences and then address your audience. This is particularly helpful if your speech is too long to memorize.

- ◆ **The Vagues.** Avoiding definitive statements, not coming to the point or saying anything of substance. *Remedy*: Give your listeners something to sink their teeth into.

  Avoid using cliches and platitudes. They may come easy, but they detract from the effectiveness of your speech. So will jargon and statistics. Nothing turns off a listener faster than long lists of figures or abstruse technical phraseology. Learn to limit your topic to what your audience needs to know and can reasonably digest.

- ◆ **The Circle Syndrome.** A loss of equilibrium causing the speaker to continually return to the point from which he or she began — usually a side effect of poor preparation. *Remedy*: The healthy speaker progresses in a straight line. Speaking in circles is a sure sign that you've lost your way and the audience will soon realize you're going nowhere.

- ◆ **Fractured Syntax.** The speaker reveals this disability and mars an otherwise good impression with a few blunders in grammar and pronunciation. *Remedy*: A booster shot of grammar. Few speakers are perfect grammarians. But it is worthwhile to avoid the more flagrant violations. The same holds true for pronunciation. When in doubt, the simple rule is, take ten seconds and look it up. Faulty grammar and pronunciation indicate that you didn't care enough to get it right.

- ◆ **Anemic Conclusion.** Failure to nurture the end of a speech as carefully as the beginning. *Remedy*: Build up and round out your conclusion. Your last statements will stay with your listeners the longest so return to your initial proposal, recap the points you've made, and tie it all together.

Few people rise to the top without cultivating public-speaking ability. So take the floor and fear not!

Stapleton Communications   **SPEAKING WITH AUTHORITY**

**"It's not what you say,
it's how you say it!"**

From the time we get up in the morning until we go to bed at night, most of us are negotiating our lives with our voices. We talk to our personal cast of characters — spouses, children, parents, friends, clients, bosses — and just how much authority we bring to all this talking determines its effectiveness.

Whatever you're trying to get across must first be heard, and nobody will really hear you unless your voice is capable of capturing attention and keeping it. *Energy* is the secret of talking effectively. It's crucial to speak out so that your listener isn't under a strain to catch your meaning. Too many people lack force and talk just at the threshhold of audibility. Others start out all right, then drop sentences to nothing.

You have to keep the energy going, because it's the key element in projecting a positive image.

Here are techniques for developing, building, and projecting an energetic voice that carries the sound of *authority*:

1) *Remember that your listeners are just people very much like you.* Consider yourself on an equal footing, then proceed to act as if you're self-assured and unafraid, even if you're not. This will help to overcome nervousness.

2) *Videotape yourself.* You get to see and hear yourself as your audience does. This is the perfect tool for in-depth self-evaluation.

3) *Get used to speaking out loud.* Practice doing so at home, to yourself, or to anyone who will listen to you. Make your voice travel forward so that it isn't swallowed and diffused. Cast your voice forward as though you were calling out to someone across the street. Be dramatic while practicing, and don't be afraid of exaggeration.

4) *Overcome rigidity.* We get set in our ways, holding ourselves in the same positions with our jaws set a certain way and our resonance chambers stuck in the same range. When we don't open our mouths to speak, we don't use our lips and jaws freely, and speech becomes slurred.

5) *Imitate role models.* Listen to the voice of someone you admire or consider "well-spoken." Analyze what you like about the way they sound. This mimicking forces different uses of the tongue, throat, jaw, and lips, and expands ability to speak with authority.

6) *Vary your speaking rate.* Change speed of sentences, from fast to slow according to what you need to emphasize. Speak quickly as you lead up to a point and then slow down to make the point.

7) *Concentrate on pitch.* A high vocal pitch is associated with childishness and immaturity and usually betrays emotional stress. Bring it down by relaxing the throat muscles and speaking as low as you can comfortably within your natural range. Although a low pitch carries conviction and authority, don't force it too far or your voice will become strained and lose flexibility.

8) *Turn up the volume.* Low volume suggests low energy, low enthusiasm, and powerlessness. Contrary to popular opinion, when you whisper or murmur, people don't lean forward to catch your every word. Instead, they lean back and stop listening. Practice raising and lowering your voice for effect, always keeping it clear and audible. The physical force it takes to increase volume will give you a sense of mastery.

The more you work on these techiques, the easier they become. You can noticeably build up your confidence and sense of authority by rehearsing in safe environments, such as oral-presentation workshops, or groups such as Toastmasters.

Practice at every opportunity until your new-found speaking skills become habitual. And remember that all habits — both good and bad — are hard to break.

Adapted from the Los Angeles Times

The Meeting Environment

While it is often difficult or impossible to control certain characteristics of your meeting environment, the room and how you choose to arrange it will have a definite effect on the outcome of your meeting.

Ideally, the size of the room should be appropriate to the number of attendees. If a room is too small, your audience will be uncomfortable, ventilation will be inadequate, and there won't be enough room if you need to move around to set up equipment or displays. If a room is too large, it can have a cold, empty feeling and the acoustics are likely to be poor.

Everyone in the room must have a clear view of the speaker as well as projected visuals and other displays. Long, narrow rooms, rooms with obstructing columns or posts, or rooms with low ceilings should be avoided. Recommended ceiling heights are ten to fifteen feet. A speaker platform should be provided if there are too many attendees to allow eye contact between the back rows and the presenter. Lights should be adequate (but never directly over a projection screen) with provisions for darkening the room if slides, movies, or filmstrips will be shown. Chairs should be comfortable and not crowded together. Adequate ventilation is very important – *concentration deteriorates in a stuffy room.* Poor acoustics are annoying and every attempt should be made to soften hard surfaces with carpeting, drapes, and acoustical tiles. Remember that acoustics improve when a room is filled with people. Room access should be limited to the rear of the room to avoid interruptions by latecomers. And, finally, be sure restroom facilities are adequate and easily accessible.

The following four room arrangements will assist you with proper speaker, audience and equipment placement.
The center table and U-shape arrangements are ideal for discussion meetings, the former best suited for under twenty people and the latter, under thirty. The classroom and auditorium arrangements are suitable for any size audience.

Center Table Arrangement

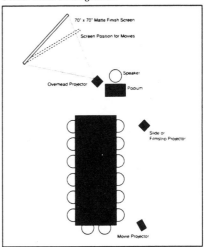

Classroom Arrangement

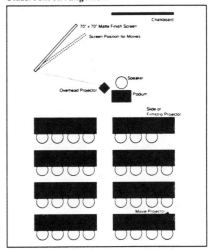

U-Shaped Table Arrangement

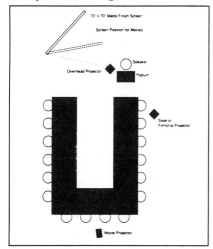

Combination U-Shape/Auditorium

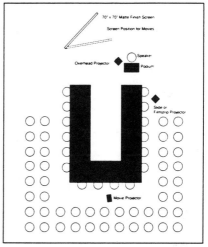

Auditorium Arrangement

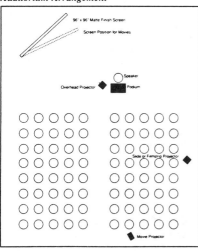

You may want to combine different aspects of these set-ups for your particular purpose. If many people are attending the meeting to hear a few discuss an issue, a U-shaped table could be placed at the front of the room with the observers seated around the sides of the room or auditorium style at the rear.

Stapleton Communications   **QUICK REFERENCE CHECKLIST**

(**HIGHLIGHTS**)

1) Define presentation content.
2) Peg your audience.
3) Pick format - "B M W".
4) Develop a presentation strategy.
5) Make your *Opening* provide a message pathway.
6) Be sure the *Body* contains detail/value.
7) Recap points and state action plan in the *Closing.*
8) Research ——► Rehearse.
9) Vocalize and Visualize.
10) Plan, Prepare, Present!

* * * * * * * *

Define Content

Is the intent to generate action or merely inform? Follow these steps:
- Know your purpose
- Use a presentation planning form
- Determine the message value
- Know how the info will be used
- Determine action responsibility

Peg Audience

Ask these questions:
- Who is the audience?
- What do they need to know?
- How will the audience react to the presentation?
- What background do they already have?
- How can I best persuade them?

Pick Format

Remember that the majority of presentations can be slotted into three categories:
- ◆ Briefing -- informal discussion, small group, short duration
- ◆ Meeting -- specific agenda, larger group, longer time
- ◆ Workshop -- training or information session/seminar

Develop Strategy

Think about the best way to individualize your presentation. What will work best in going about how you assemble the material? How can you target to this particular group of listeners? What will you have to do to spark and maintain interest?

| *Stapleton Communications* | QUICK REFERENCE CHECKLIST |

Structure the Opening

An effectively prepared presentation opening sets the tone and provides a pathway through the rest of your message. Generally, your opening comments will work best when they contain a presentation overview combined with an emphatic approach.

Structure the Body

Using the presentation planning form, give the details of your presentation a logical flow. Consider how visual aids can assist in getting your message across in an appealing way. Be certain to include the value-added content of your presentation.

Structure the Closing

Your presentation closing will have impact for your audience when you include a recap of main points made and tell what happens next. Are you making an action plan clear to your listeners? Remember that the audience is wondering, "Where do we go from here?"

Research ⟶ Rehearse

Follow this process:
- Assemble your material
- Use the presentation planning form to lay out your message
- Dry run, being sure to time your presentation, check visual aid use, and practice your projection style

Vocalize & Visualize

Speak up and speak out. Pay attention to vocal inflection and intonation. Be aware of your movement, posture, gestures, and energy! Remember the do's & don'ts.

Plan, Prepare, Present!

Pull it all together to project the image of you which puts your best foot forward.

If you'd like to pursue further some of the ideas for improvement presented in this book, here's a list of suggested readings, software programs, and hardware which you'll find of great help.

Books

A Grammar of the English Language. Curme: Verbatim.

American Heritage Dictionary, 5th ed.: Dell Publishing.

Business Writer's Handbook. Brusaw, Alred & Oliu: St. Martin's.

Dress For Success. Molloy: Warner Books.

Elements of Style. Strunk & White: MacMillan.

Essentials of English, 4th ed.: Barron's Educational Series.

Handbook of Technical Writing. Brusaw, Alred & Oliu: St. Martin's.

Hodges' Harbrace College Handbook, 11th ed.: HBJ Publishers.

How to Prepare, Stage and Deliver A Winning Presentation. Leech: Amacom.

How to Write & Publish a Scientific Paper. Day: Oryx Press.

How to Write and Speak in Business. Kaumeyer: Coleman and Associates.

Let's Talk. Sathré-Eldon, Olson, and Whitney: Scott, Foresman and Co.

Lions Don't Need to Roar. Benton: Warner Books.

<u>Miss Thistlebottom's Hobgoblins</u>. Bernstein:
Farrar, Straus and Giroux.

<u>Modern English Usage</u>. Fowler: Oxford
University Press.

<u>On Writing Well</u>. Zinsser: Harper & Row.

<u>Reading, Writing, Thinking</u>. Lawrence: Charles
Scribner's Sons.

<u>Roget's Thesaurus</u>. T.Y. Crowel Co.

<u>Six Minutes a Day to Perfect Spelling</u>. Shefter:
Simon & Schuster.

<u>Speak Easy: 101 Ways to Think on Your Feet Without
Falling Flat on Your Face</u>. Osgood: Morrow.

<u>Stress Training for Life</u>. Kindler: Nichols.

<u>Technical Writing Situations & Strategies</u>. Markel:
St. Martin's.

<u>The Deluxe Transitive Vampire</u>. Gordon:
Pantheon.

<u>The Elements of Speechwriting and Public
Speaking</u>. Cook: Collier Books.

<u>The New Well-Tempered Sentence</u>. Gordon:
Ticknor & Fields.

<u>The Persuasive Presentation</u>. Goodall and
Waagen: Harper & Row.

<u>30 Days to Better English</u>. Lewis: Signet.

<u>US News Stylebook</u>, US News & World Report.

<u>Webster's Dictionary of English Usage.</u> Merriam–
Webster.

Software

<u>Grammatik</u> (PC & Mac)

<u>RightWriter</u> (PC & Mac)

<u>Sensible Grammar</u> (Mac)

Spelling improvement:
    <u>Spell Dodger!</u> (Davidson – Mac)
    <u>Word Attack 3</u> (Davidson – PC)

Hardware

Franklin Language Master

Franklin Word Master

Contents

A good point to remember about abbreviations: avoid them unless the abbreviation is a conventional one that is readily recognized by the reader. To prevent misunderstandings, it is preferable <u>not</u> to abbreviate in text. In figures and tables it is expedient to do so for conformity's sake, since there is not always room to spell everything out.

GENERAL RULES FOR ABBREVIATING

- Abbreviate units of measure only if they are preceded by numerals:

    9 in.; *but*, several inches

- Place Latin abbreviations in parentheses:

    (e.g., like this example)   (i.e., in other words)

- Write numbers combined with abbreviations with a space, except when the abbreviation consists of only one letter:

    100 psi, 1200 rpm, 5V

- Use the same abbreviation for singular and plural forms:

    lb., *not* lbs; yd., *not* yds

- Use the slash mark (/) for "per" in compound abbreviations that have no established short form:

    lb./sec.   ft./min.

- Omit "No." for "Number" whenever possible:

    Engines 1 and 2; *but* the No. 2 engine (as a descriptive designation)

- Use USPS abbreviations for states:

    CA NY ME AL

- Do not abbreviate:

    — Three-letter words

    — Days of week or months of year except in figures or tables

    — At the beginning of a sentence, with the exception of a title (Dr.; Mr.)

- Punctuate abbreviations when:

    — The abbreviation forms a word: C.O.D.; in.

    — The form is taken from Latin: i.e.; e.g.; etc.

    — Conventional use demands:
      B.A.; Ph.D.; Mr.; Mrs.; p.; U.S.A.; D.C. (the district)

ACCEPTABLE ABBREVIATIONS IN TEXT

Dr.	A.A.	Associate of Arts
Mr.	B.A.	Bachelor of Arts
Mrs.	B.S.	Bachelor of Science
Ms.	D.S.	Doctor of Science
Messrs.	M.A.	Master of Arts
Jr.	M.S.	Master of Science
Sr.	Ph.D.	Doctor of Philosophy
Esq.	D. Lit.	Doctor of Letters
TV	M.D.	Doctor of Medicine
FBI	LL.D.	Doctor of Laws
U.S.A.	B.C.	Before Christ
U.N. delegation (as adjective)	A.D.	anno Domini
U.S. delegation (as adjective)	a.m.	ante meridian
the United States (used as a noun)	p.m.	post meridian

Bullets, numbers, and letters may be used to set off items or paragraphs in text. This use is essential to "Content Mapping." Here are examples:

BULLETS

• To set off a long series of statements that would otherwise create an awkward sentence

• To list a series of items

• To set off short paragraphs for emphasis

• To identify paragraphs when paragraph numbers or heading variations have been exhausted

    Format Suggestions (may vary according to personal preference):

• Indent bullet from left-hand margin.

    — Use a dash for second indentation.

      * Use an asterisk for third indentation.

• Put a period at end of item when writing a complete sentence.

NUMBERS & LETTERS

1. To list procedural steps in sequence

2. To establish priority

3. To list items that will be referred to by number later in the text (for correlation purposes)

    Format Suggestions (may vary according to personal preference):

1. Indent numbers from left-hand margin.

    a. Use a lower-case letter for second indentation.

      (1) Use number in parenthesis for third indentation.

2. Put a period at end of item when writing a complete sentence.

Checklist for when to use capital letters:

- Use them sparingly. When in doubt, do not capitalize.

- Titles and Offices:

Lower Case	Capitalize
government	U.S. Government
chief deputy	Chief Deputy Smith
accounting studies	studies by Accounting
value engineering	Value Engineering Dept.
mayor of Los Angeles	Mayor Richard Riordan
department manager	Department Manager Jones

- Acronyms — Do not capitalize words unless they are proper nouns:

Phrase	Acronym
automated teller machine	ATM
electronic countermeasure	ECM
integrated logistics support	ILS
inertial measurement unit	IMU
maintainance parts list	MPL
quick engine change	QEC

- Acronyms for units of measurement are generally lower case:

revolutions per minute	rpm
pounds per square inch	psi
kips per square inch	ksi

- Military terms and titles:

Fifth Fleet   World War II   Chinese Army

Army
Navy
Air Force
Marines

- Government departments and offices:

  Senate
  House of Representatives
  Supreme Court
  Court of Appeals

- Trade names:

  Kevlar
  Dacron
  Plexiglas
  Foamite

- Names of races, languages, religions:

  Caucasian, Mongolian, Protestant, Jewish, Indian, English

  but

  blacks and whites
  black entrepreneurs
  white storekeepers

- North, south, east, and west when they are:

Regions	*Proper Nouns*
mysterious East	West Side
new Southwest	East Lansing

- Complete names of churches, rivers, hotels:

  First Baptist Church
  Mark Hopkins Hotel
  Mississippi River

Editing comprises preparing a writer's work for publication by pointing out where revision is necessary to ready the text. Editing *may* involve rewriting, but is generally a review process. The purposes of editing are to ensure adherence to grammar rules, ensure that copy is in the required format, and ensure that the information is presented as clearly as possible. The function of the editor is to help the writer communicate effectively. Below is a checklist of steps to aid in carrying out the editor's responsibilities:

1. SECTION CONSISTENCY

- Does each section have a title or heading?
- Does each section contain an introductory paragraph?
- Are all sections organized in the same manner?

2. OVERALL CONSISTENCY

- Does the document read as a unified whole?
- Is the style of presentation uniform or disjointed?
- Do sections flow from one to another?

3. ABBREVIATIONS/ACRONYMS

- Is usage consistent throughout the text?
- Are abbreviations and acronyms defined?
- Is punctuation correct?

4. CAPITALIZING

- Are capital letters used consistently throughout the document?

5. NUMBERS

- Are Arabic numbers preferred and used uniformly?
- Are decimals guarded (0.75, 0.01)?
- Are numbers tabulated where possible?

6. RECOMMENDATIONS

- Are they clear and concise?
- Are they supported by facts, data, and analyses in the document?
- Are they presented at the end of each section or combined at the end of the document?

7. FIGURES AND TABLES

- Are they called out in text?
- Do figures and tables match callouts?
- Do table captions explain thoroughly and have a "stand alone" quality?
- Are they numbered correctly in sequence?

8. REFERENCES

- Are all references called out in text?
- Are they numbered in order of presentation?
- Have they all been listed in the reference list?
- Are all cross references to sections, paragraphs, and pages correct?

9. APPENDICES/EXHIBITS

- Are they listed or numbered consecutively?
- Do figures and tables carry proper designation?
- Are pages numbered with proper designation?

Editor's Checklist (cont.)

When a document is offered for technical review, the editor assumes it to be complete and ready for publication (i.e., ready for word processing and any graphics), subject to formal approval. The editor must first determine whether:

a. On technical grounds, no bar exists to publication
b. On technical grounds, no bar exists to publication provided certain specific changes are made

The editor is responsible for assessing the technical quality of the work, including assumptions, matters of fact, logic of development, quality of analysis, and soundness of conclusions. The accuracy of major numerical results is checked and a spot check is made on the accuracy of tables and figures. Here are technical review guidelines for editors (particularly helpful for reports):

1. ORGANIZATION

Is the material easily followed throughout? If not, how can it be reorganized? Refer to sections and page numbers as necessary.

2. INTRODUCTION

Does the writer clearly explain the purpose and nature of the inquiry, the method used, and the limiting assumptions or other constraints? Suggest specific appropriate improvements.

3. CONCLUSIONS

Are the conclusions adequately supported by the preceding data and analysis, and are they so stated as to be clear and helpful? Keep in mind that reports are generally intended for specific audiences.

4. SECTION-BY-SECTION ANALYSIS

Refer to page numbers and point out possible errors, obscurities, or misinterpretations. Suggest specific ways of improving the text. Mark the review copy to indicate any misspellings or typographical errors. Mark tables and figures to designate how they could be improved.

Mark	Meaning	Mark	Meaning
ℰ	delete	*stet*	let it stand
∧	insert	¶	begin new paragraph
∿	transpose	⫫	no paragraph
/	make lower case	⟶	indent
=	make capitals	⟵	move to left margin
⌣	close up	⟷	delete space between words
|	insert space		
⊙	insert period	C ℓ	start with capitals, followed by lower case
⊚	insert comma	⊂⊃	insert dash
⊙	insert semicolon		
⊙	insert colon	⊘	insert quotation marks
⊖	insert hyphen	⊘	insert single quotes (or apostrophe)

Plus —

Word circled - usage questioned: (malicious)software

Verb underlined - passive voice: *fraud was found*

Sentence notations in margin: "Long" (exceeds 20 words)
"Periodic" (main idea at end)

Paragraph notations in margin: "Dense" (exceeds 5 sentences)
"Subheads" (use Content Mapping)

Grammar means the system of rules or guidelines we use to communicate intelligibly and uniformly. Though the word may have a somewhat stodgy connotation, grammar is actually vital, and constantly evolving. To fix it would be to kill it.

While you probably do not need to know the difference between a correlative conjunction and an asyndetic clause, knowledge of some grammar basics — specifically, what to watch for — can be helpful in your business writing:

• etc.	Avoid using because it is vague. Use more complete, detailed terms.
• however therefore also thus hence	These transitional words are important to the flow of text. They serve as linking devices. (See page 85 for more.)
• obvious well known readily apparent of course clearly	These terms may insult readers. What you are writing about may or may not be "obvious." Let the reader decide.
• type	Avoid expressions like: conventional-type wheels; automatic-type transmission.
• the Company	Avoid this in typical writing. It is a contractual expression, but not apropos. Use "we" or your company name instead.
• data	Singular or plural verb required? The debate rages. Check your reference. "This data" would be followed by "is"; "these data" by "are."
• don't won't can't isn't	Avoid contractions in technical or highly formal writing. They tend to sound too chummy.

- Use the indefinite article "a" . . .

. . . when an abbreviation begins with b, c, d, g, j, k, p, q, t, u, v, w, y, or z, each having a consonant sound. Examples: a CRT display, a DC motor, a UHF antenna.

- Use the indefinite article "an" . . .

. . . when an abbreviation begins with a, e, f, h, i, l, m, n, o, r, s, or x, each having a vowel sound. Examples: an AC motor, an EGT reading, an RPM indication.

- Figure and table references

Use "in" — not "on" — when referring to a figure or table.

As shown in Figure 9.
Listed in Table 15.

In text, write references into sentences rather than inserting into parenthesis.
Avoid "(see Figure 8)."
Prefer "See Figure 8 for test results."

Parallel Construction

Parallel construction means that a train of equivalent ideas or a series are of the same grammatical genre — in other words, message elements are uniform and consistent in part-of-speech usage.

Guidelines, with examples:

- Repeat parallel connectives:

    "By weeks of careful planning, by intelligence, by training, and by a great deal of luck . . . "

    "A nut, a bolt, a hammer, and a screwdriver."

- Parallel pairs (*correct version is in parenthesis*):

    "They accepted the design and scheduling (the design and schedule)."

    "They wanted peace without being dishonored (peace without dishonor)."

- Parallel coordinators — Be sure to put them in the right place:

    "Either he is an engineer or a draftsman."

    "Neither in time nor space . . . "

    "We not only like the design, but also the color scheme."

- Parallel numerical coordinators:

    "For a number of reasons we decided: 1) that it was too costly; 2) that it would not work."

    "My objections are that:
        1) As a consultant, he charges too much
        2) As an Armed Forces member, he represents a conflict of interest "

◆ Parallel listed items:

Poor	Better
- Outsize capable	- Is outsize capable
- Completes 180-degree turn with 86 feet	- Can complete a 180-degree turn within 86 feet
- 2.5 percent grade backup	- Can back up a 2.5 percent grade

The two best aides for spelling are a dictionary and a software spellcheck program. If you think speling dusunt matar, just try reeding the remanedur uv the wurds in thiss sentunce withowt lozing spede and kompreehenshun.

Here are three underlying principles of good spelling:

- ◆ Pronunciation can help you spell. If you pronounce a word correctly, chances are you will spell it correctly. (Beware the exceptions like *Wednesday* and *phlegm.*)

- ◆ The rule of "i" before "e":

> I before e
> Except after c
> Or when sounded like a
> As in neighbor and weigh.

- ◆ Most sesquipedalian words derived from the Latin or French form spell their sounds letter for letter. The common Latin prefixes (and their assimilations) account for the double consonants at the first syllabic joint of so many of our words:

> AD (ab, ac): abbreviate, accept
> CON (col, com): collapse, commit
> DIS (apart): dissect, dissolve
> IN (il): illuminate, illusion
> INTER (between): interrupt, interrogate
> OB (oc, op): occupy, oppose
> SUB (suf, sup): suffer, suppose
> SYN (syl, sym): syllable, symmetry [Greek]

Software tutorials, listed under **Resources** *(page 155), are also available to help you improve spelling:*

> * Spell Dodger! (Davidson – Mac)

> * Word Attack 3 (Davidson – PC)

Tense

No need to get tense about this topic. And be careful not to confuse *past tense* with *passive voice*. The two have nothing to do with one another. A verb can be in passive voice but future tense ("Directives <u>must be followed</u> as written").

Tense has to do with the chronological condition described by the verb — the time distinction. Base your choice of appropriate tense on the following:

- **Past tense:**   To define conditions or events which have occurred [Signal: "d" or "ed" verb endings]

- **Present tense:**   Statements of fact
  Existing conditions
  Permanently true conditions
  Suggested alternative approach

- **Future tense:**   Future conditions (work phases to be accomplished)
  What work will be done
  Steps to be taken
  Techniques to be used
  Conditional situations

As a general rule of thumb, prefer the present tense throughout reports, unless you are writing about events or conditions which are over and done with.

Check for unintentional shifts in tense. These are examples of the *tennis-match syndrome*:

Change: Before Vinnie *called* on the delinquent payment, he *made* sure the client *understands* the problem.

To: Before Vinnie *called* on the delinquent payment, he *made* sure the client *understood* the problem.

Verbosity

In the give-and-take of conversation, we are apt to repeat ourselves and to use words that are meaningless or unnecessary. When writing we have the opportunity to go over our work and remove the verbosity. These suggestions may be helpful:

- Avoid using two or more words where one will serve better:

    Wordy: Cease and desist.
    Concise: Stop.

    Wordy: It is the belief of the Managers . . .
    Concise: The Managers believe . . .

    Wordy: The car is green in color.
    Concise: The car is green.

- Avoid adding words to an idea already expressed. Examples are:

    — Using "again" with verbs beginning with "re-"
    — Using "more" or "most" with adjectives and adverbs ending in "-er" and "-est"
    — Using "more" or "most" with absolute-meaning adjectives such as unique, round, square, and equal

SAMPLE VERBOSE EXPRESSIONS

absolutely essential
audible to the ear
call on the phone
close proximity
completely unanimous
connect up with
consensus of opinion
cooperate together
each and every one
endorse on the back
few (many) in number
first beginnings
fundamental principles
important essentials
join together

more perfect
most unique
old adage
personal friend
recur again
refer back
rise up
round in form
separate out
small in size
talented genius
this afternoon at 4 p.m.
this morning at 8 a.m.
visible to the eye

About the Author

Tom Stapleton is a freelance writer and communications consultant. His clients include corporations and government agencies. He has written a variety of magazine articles and newspaper feature pieces for publications such as Ladies Home Journal, The Los Angeles Times, The Denver Post, *and* Entrepreneur Magazine.

As a trainer, Tom has conducted business writing and oral presentations workshops for numerous organizations, among them Amgen, The Walt Disney Company, Northrop Grumman, Nestlé, Pharmavite, Los Angeles County, Florida Dept. of Law Enforcement, and the U.S. Dept. of Transportation.

He has taught business writing courses at Caltech and UCLA Extension. Tom earned his master's degree in English at the University of Colorado.